WORLD HISTORY SERIES ■ ■ ■

The Conquest of Mexico

Titles in the World History Series

The Age of Augustus
The Age of Feudalism
The Age of Pericles
The American Frontier
The American Revolution
Ancient Greece
The Ancient Near East
Architecture
Aztec Civilization
The Black Death
The Byzantine Empire
Caesar's Conquest of Gaul
The California Gold Rush
The Chinese Cultural
    Revolution
The Conquest of Mexico
The Crusades
The Cuban Revolution
The Early Middle Ages
Egypt of the Pharaohs
Elizabethan England
The End of the Cold War
The French and Indian War
The French Revolution
The Glorious Revolution
The Great Depression

Greek and Roman Theater
Hitler's Reich
The Hundred Years' War
The Inquisition
The Italian Renaissance
The Late Middle Ages
The Lewis and Clark
    Expedition
The Mexican Revolution
The Mexican War of
    Independence
Modern Japan
The Punic Wars
The Reformation
The Relocation of the
    North American Indian
The Roman Empire
The Roman Republic
The Russian Revolution
The Scientific Revolution
The Spread of Islam
Traditional Africa
Traditional Japan
The Travels of Marco Polo
The Wars of the Roses
Women's Suffrage

WORLD
HISTORY SERIES ▪▪▪

The Conquest
of Mexico

by
Stephen R. Lilley

Lucent Books, P.O. Box 289011, San Diego, CA 92198-9011

Library of Congress Cataloging-in-Publication Data

Lilley, Stephen R., 1950–
    The conquest of Mexico / by Stephen R. Lilley.
      p. cm.—(World history series)
    Includes bibliographical references and index.
    Summary: Examines the Spanish conquest of Mexico in
1521 which brought together two cultures that had been
developing independently for at least 750 generations.
    ISBN 1-56006-298-3 (alk. paper)
    1. Mexico—History—Conquest, 1519–1540—Juvenile
literature. [1. Mexico—History—Conquest, 1519–1540.]
I. Title. II. Series.
F1230.L55   1997
972'.02—dc20   96–21506
                                 CIP
                                 AC

Copyright 1997 by Lucent Books, Inc., P.O. Box 289011,
San Diego, California 92198-9011

Printed in the U.S.A.

Contents

Foreword

Each year on the first day of school, nearly every history teacher faces the task of explaining why his or her students should study history. One logical answer to this question is that exploring what happened in our past explains how the things we often take for granted—our customs, ideas, and institutions—came to be. As statesman and historian Winston Churchill put it, "Every nation or group of nations has its own tale to tell. Knowledge of the trials and struggles is necessary to all who would comprehend the problems, perils, challenges, and opportunities which confront us today." Thus, a study of history puts modern ideas and institutions in perspective. For example, though the founders of the United States were talented and creative thinkers, they clearly did not invent the concept of democracy. Instead, they adapted some democratic ideas that had originated in ancient Greece and with which the Romans, the British, and others had experimented. An exploration of these cultures, then, reveals their very real connection to us through institutions that continue to shape our daily lives.

Another reason often given for studying history is the idea that lessons exist in the past from which contemporary societies can benefit and learn. This idea, although controversial, has always been an intriguing one for historians. Those that agree that society can benefit from the past often quote philosopher George Santayana's famous statement, "Those who cannot remember the past are condemned to repeat it." Historians who ascribe to Santayana's philosophy believe that, for example, studying the events that led up to the major world wars or other significant historical events would allow society to chart a different and more favorable course in the future.

Just as difficult as convincing students to realize the importance of studying history is the search for useful and interesting supplementary materials that present historical events in a context that can be easily understood. The volumes in Lucent Books' World History Series attempt to present a broad, balanced, and penetrating view of the march of history. Ancient Egypt's important wars and rulers, for example, are presented against the rich and colorful backdrop of Egyptian religious, social, and cultural developments. The series engages the reader by enhancing historical events with these cultural contexts. For example, in *Ancient Greece*, the text covers the role of women in that society. Slavery is discussed in *The Roman Empire*, as well as how slaves earned their freedom. The numerous and varied aspects of everyday life in these and other societies are explored in each volume of the series. Additionally, the series covers the major political, cultural, and philosophical ideas as the torch of civilization is passed from ancient Mesopotamia and Egypt, through Greece, Rome, Medieval Europe, and other world cultures, to the modern day.

The material in the series is formatted in a thorough, precise, and organized manner. Each volume offers the reader a comprehensive and clearly written overview of an important historical event or period. The topic under discussion is placed in a broad historical context. For example, *The Italian Renaissance* begins with a discussion of the High Middle Ages and the loss of central control that allowed certain Italian cities to develop artistically. The book ends by looking forward to the Reformation and interpreting the societal changes that grew out of the Renaissance. Thus, students are not only involved in an historical era, but also enveloped by the events leading up to that era and the events following it.

One important and unique feature in the World History Series is the primary and secondary source quotations that richly supplement each volume. These quotes are useful in a number of ways. First, they allow students access to sources they would not normally be exposed to because of the difficulty and obscurity of the original source. The quotations range from interesting anecdotes to farsighted cultural perspectives and are drawn from historical witnesses both past and present. Second, the quotes demonstrate how and where historians themselves derive their information on the past as they strive to reach a consensus on historical events. Lastly, all of the quotes are footnoted, familiarizing students with the citation process and allowing them to verify quotes and/or look up the original source if the quote piques their interest.

Finally, the books in the World History Series provide a detailed launching point for further research. Each book contains a bibliography specifically geared toward student research. A second, annotated bibliography introduces students to all the sources the author consulted when compiling the book. A chronology of important dates gives students an overview, at a glance, of the topic covered. Where applicable, a glossary of terms is included.

In short, the series is designed not only to acquaint readers with the basics of history, but also to make them aware that their lives are a part of an ongoing human saga. Perhaps they will then come to the same realization as famed historian Arnold Toynbee. In his monumental work, *A Study of History,* he wrote about becoming aware of history flowing through him in a mighty current, and of his own life "welling like a wave in the flow of this vast tide."

Important Dates in the Conquest of Mexico

1325	1502	1503	1511	1517	1518	1519	1520

1325
Aztecs found Tenochtitlán.

1502
Queen Isabella of Spain orders conquered Indians to be well treated. Sets up *encomienda* system.

1503
Montezuma becomes Aztec ruler, a position he holds until his death during the Spanish occupation of Tenochtitlán.

1511
Diego Velázquez leads a Spanish army that conquers Cuba.

1517
Francisco Fernández de Córdoba sails west from Cuba searching for new lands. Landing in Yucatán, he discovers advanced Indian peoples, but Córdoba and half his men die in battles with the natives.

1518
Cuba's governor, Diego Velázquez, sends Juan de Grijalva with an expedition to Yucatán. Grijalva returns to Cuba with gold obtained in trade but many of his men are killed fighting Yucatán's natives. Velázquez names Hernando Cortés to command expedition to Yucatán.

1519
Cortés leads Spanish expedition to Yucatán. He defeats the coastal Indians and Tlaxcalans and persuades many natives to join him against the Aztecs. The Spanish army enters Tenochtitlán.

1520
Cortés and his men retreat from Tenochtitlán, suffering heavy losses. The Spaniards defeat a large Aztec army at the Battle of Otumba. Smallpox contracted from the Spaniards decimates the Aztec population.

Montezuma dies. Cuauhtemoc becomes Aztec king at age eighteen.

King Charles I outlaws *encomiendas*.

1521

Having rebuilt their army and assembled a large force of Indian allies, Cortés and his men destroy Tenochtitlán and build Mexico City on its ruins.

1525

Cortés executes Cuauhtemoc, the last of the Aztec emperors.

1528

Cortés returns to Spain asking King Charles I to name him governor of New Spain.

1529

Charles I declares Cortés Captain-General of New Spain and Marquess of the Valley of Oaxaca but does not appoint him governor as he had requested.

1531

An Indian named Juan Diego reports the miraculous appearance of the Virgin of Guadalupe.

1537

Pope Paul III declares Indians are not to be enslaved and that they have property rights.

1545

Charles I declares *encomiendas* may be inherited.

1547

While in Spain to see Charles I, Cortés dies near Seville. His body is returned to Mexico for burial.

When Cultures Collide

The Spanish conquest of Mexico in 1521 brought together two cultures that had been developing independently for at least 750 generations. The ancestors of the Aztecs (or "Mexica" as they called them-

The meeting of the emperor Montezuma and Cortés would have international repercussions and lead to the destruction of the Aztec culture.

selves) probably left Asia as much as nineteen thousand years before humans kept written records of their activities. The ancestors of the Spaniards included the Celts and Greeks from Europe and the Phoenicians from northern Africa. The Spaniards developed in a European crossroads eventually dominated by the Romans and still later the Moslems from Africa. When the Aztecs and Spaniards met on the shore of the Gulf of Mexico, the long separation of time and geography had made them very different. While, like all humans, they shared common traits, even their similarities helped to make them enemies.

Both societies had developed in poor lands that bred hardy, ambitious warriors. Both were ruled by increasingly powerful hereditary monarchs. Both kingdoms were approaching the peaks of their military and political power. And both societies followed religions that demanded much of their resources and all of their loyalty. Each spread its religion and its way of life to its neighbors by war. Eventually the two expanding empires collided. Neither society clearly foresaw the consequences their conquests would bring.

One clear consequence was that neither empire ever lacked enemies. As the Aztecs expanded their domain, their violence, oppression, and greed made ene-

A Nineteenth-Century Defense of the Conquest

While acknowledging Spanish cruelty during the conquest, nineteenth-century historian William H. Prescott, in this excerpt from his Conquest of Mexico, *found little to admire in the Aztecs' treatment of their subjects.*

"We cannot regret the fall of an empire which did so little to promote the happiness of its subjects, or the real interests of humanity. . . . The Aztecs were . . . a fierce and brutal race, little calculated, in their best aspects to excite our sympathy and regard. . . . They ruled over their wide domains with a sword instead of a sceptre. . . . Their vassals were serfs, used only to minister to their pleasure, held in awe by armed garrisons, ground to the dust by imposts [taxes] in peace, by military conscriptions in war. . . . They did not amalgamate [join] them into one great nation, with common rights and interests. They held them as aliens—even those who in the valley were gathered round the very walls of the capital. The Aztec metropolis [Tenochtitlán] had not a sympathy, not a pulsation, in common with the rest of the body politic [the people it governed]. It was a stranger in its own land."

mies of every group they encountered. To the Aztecs there were two kinds of people: those they had conquered and those they expected to conquer. By the time the white-skinned strangers landed in Yucatán, the subject peoples of Mexico were prepared to throw off their Aztec overlords even at the price of accepting new masters. As Hubert Herring writes:

The Aztecs terrorized their subjects into submission, collected tribute from them, but made no attempt to integrate them into the Aztec nation. The vanquished peoples remained vassals [people who owe service to rulers], with only hatred in their hearts for their conquerors.[1]

The Aztecs' conquests had both given them control over Mexico and provided the Spanish invaders with willing allies in the conquest.

For their part, the Spaniards' European wars helped motivate them to cross the Atlantic in search of resources to strengthen Spain militarily. The conquistadors' prayers for success could not have been answered more to their liking. In short order, a handful of adventurers from a poor nation conquered a great empire of mythic splendor, beauty, and wealth. Not only did the conquered Indians surrender completely, but they embraced Catholicism by the millions. As the new land fell under Spanish sway, treasure ships brought gold plundered from the Indians to enrich Spain's king.

The Spaniards conquer Tenochtitlán and with it the Aztec empire. The Spaniards would rebuild Aztec cities such as Tenochtitlán after those of European design.

In the end, the two cultures became one. The Mexico of the Aztecs gave way to New Spain, the Mexico of the Spaniards. Only remnants of Aztec culture survived the conquest. European diseases in the American environment proved more deadly than they had been in the Old World, and Indians died by the millions. A new people, a blend of European and Indian (mestizos) emerged to populate the land, and this new population was overwhelmingly Catholic. However sincere their conversion, the Indians, once under Spanish control, abandoned their practice of large-scale human sacrifice. Under Spanish supervision Indian laborers demolished the great temples and palaces of the Aztec capital, Tenochtitlán, and replaced them with structures of European design. With each passing generation the Mexicans who spoke of the conquest and the times following it spoke increasingly in Spanish, not the Nahuatl language of the Aztecs. The Spaniards and their Indian subjects labored mightily to remake the new land in the Spanish image. In the end, they created a new Mexico—overpopulated, impoverished, and resentful of things European.

Obviously, this clash of cultures did not create a new culture that pleased everyone. With good reason critics have condemned the conquest and its results for over four centuries. After all, the conquistadors seized land, slaves, and gold, and felt justified in doing so. To them this was part of God's plan to Christianize the Indians. Seen in this way, the conquest was right and necessary, the stuff of legends. To Bartolomé de Las Casas, a Spanish Catholic priest who attempted to defend the Indians from abuse during the early sixteenth century, the conquest was immoral and unjust.

Las Casas was less willing to admit the Aztec empire's evils. They, too, had seized land, slaves, and gold. They also felt their gods gave them the right to slaughter their neighbors by the thousands. Unlike the Spaniards, the Aztecs encountered a

Las Casas Criticizes the Conquest

The Spanish priest Bartolomé de Las Casas defended the Indians of the New World so vigorously he became known as the Apostle of the Indies. His writings, such as this excerpt from The Devastation of the Indies: A Brief Account, *translated by Herme Briffault, painted a stereotype of Spanish cruelty that endured for centuries.*

"In the year one thousand five hundred and seven New Spain was discovered and during the discovery great outrages were perpetrated against the Indians and some of the discoverers were slain. In the year one thousand five hundred and eighteen, Spaniards who called themselves Christians went there to massacre and kill, although they said their aim was to settle Christians in the province. And from that year to this day [1542], the climax of injustice and violence and tyranny committed against the Indians has been reached and surpassed. Because the Spaniards have now lost all fear of God and King, they have ceased to know right from wrong. . . . They have committed and continue to commit . . . many acts of cruelty, . . . terrible ravages, massacres, destructions, exterminations, thefts, violences and tyrannies of all kinds. . . . From the beginning the Spaniards have always continually increased and expanded their infernal acts and outrages."

Bartolomé de Las Casas witnessed and wrote a detailed account of the cruelty the Indians experienced at the hands of the Spaniards.

conqueror who quickly overpowered them and violently suppressed their culture. It is this violent suppression of Aztec culture that has caused many to condemn the conquest.

Many modern social scientists believe that all cultures are equally good and that no society has a right to impose its values on another. To them, the Spanish conquest of the Aztec empire was a crime. This attitude would confuse or anger both the Spaniards and the Aztecs. Both believed that when cultures collide there can be only one winner.

Toward the Setting Sun

Chapter

1

By 1517, the Caribbean Sea was a Spanish lake. In four voyages between 1492 and 1504, Christopher Columbus had reached as far west as Venezuela and as far north as Honduras. He had sailed to Cuba, turned eastward, and planted a durable, if troubled, colony on the island of Hispaniola (the island now shared by Haiti and the Dominican Republic). Droves of hearty Spanish explorers and settlers followed in his wake. Some came to convert the natives to Catholicism.

In their lust for profit, ambitious Spanish settlers worked countless Indians to death, and European diseases to which the natives had no immunity killed still more. With the best land on Hispaniola already occupied and the gold mines yielding little, adventurers seeking their fortunes looked westward. In 1511, Spanish forces com-

In this traditional illustration, Columbus proudly claims the New World for Spain as a fellow sailor thanks God for his safe arrival.

manded by Diego Velázquez conquered Cuba, and the pattern of colonization in Hispaniola repeated itself. As the new governor of Cuba, Velázquez parceled out land and Indian laborers to friends, family, and faithful servants. While Cuba boasted rich land and its gold mines proved more profitable than those on Hispaniola, Indians there also died from overwork or fled to the mountains to avoid forced labor.

Córdoba Sails West

Not only did the Cuban natives resist service to their new white masters, disease, forced labor, and attacks by the Spanish drove them to the brink of extinction. At the same time, more and more ambitious young men arrived in Cuba only to find the best land occupied and Indian laborers scarce. One such group, led by a Spanish nobleman named Francisco Fernández de Córdoba, decided to seek new lands to the west where they might make their fortunes. Fortunately for historians, Bernal Díaz del Castillo was among them. Díaz left a remarkable eyewitness account of the conquest of Mexico. The son of a well-respected family, the twenty-five-year-old Díaz hungered for adventure and riches. His parents were noted for their loyalty to Spain's joint monarchs, Ferdinand and Isabella, but had little wealth to show for it. Having spent three profitless years between Tierra Firme (roughly modern Panama, Colombia, and Venezuela) and Cuba, Díaz and 108 other adventurers threw in their lot with Córdoba. Together they purchased three small ships and provisioned them for their trip into the unknown. Velázquez, eager to find a new

source of profit, sold the adventurers a small ship on credit and urged them to raid the Caribbean islands for Indian slaves who could be sold to settle the debt. In his book *The Discovery and Conquest of Mexico: 1517–1521*, Díaz claimed he and his companions objected to Velázquez's suggestion on moral grounds.

> We purchased three ships, two of them of good capacity, and the third, a bark [in the sixteenth century, any small sailing ship], bought on credit from the Governor, Diego Velázquez, on the condition that all of us soldiers should go in the three vessels to some islands lying between Cuba and Honduras . . . and make war on the natives and load the vessels with Indians, as slaves, with which to pay. . . . However, as we soldiers knew that what Diego Velásquez asked of us was not just, we answered that it was neither in accordance with the law of God nor of the king, that we should make free men slaves. When he saw that we had made up our minds, he said that our plan to go and discover new countries was better than his, and he helped us in providing food for our voyage.[2]

On February 8, 1517, Córdoba's fleet left Cuba sailing west with no real knowledge of the waters. Soon after sailing, a storm savaged the Spaniards for two days. Twenty-one days after their departure, the conquistadors sighted a land previously unknown to them, the area now known as the Yucatán Peninsula. Sailing along the coast, they saw a town with pyramids so tall they were visible from the sea even though Díaz estimated the site stood five miles from the shoreline. The Spaniards, who in Hispaniola and Cuba had seen only modest

Córdoba Sails into the Unknown

In their trip to Yucatán, Córdoba and his men risked their investments and their lives on little more than the hope they would find rich lands. In his Discovery and Conquest of Mexico: 1517–1521, *Bernal Díaz del Castillo described their plunge into the unknown.*

"On the eighth day of the month of February in the year fifteen hundred and seventeen, we left the port on the North coast [of Cuba]. . . . When we . . . were in the open sea . . . trusting to luck we steered towards the setting sun, knowing nothing of the depth of water, nor of the currents, nor of the winds which usually prevail in that latitude, so we ran great risk of our lives, when a storm struck us which lasted two days and two nights, and raged with such strength that we were nearly lost. When the weather moderated, we kept on our course, and twenty-one days after leaving port, we sighted land, at which we rejoiced greatly and gave thanks to God. This land had never been discovered before, and no report of it had reached us. From the ships we could see a large town standing back about two leagues [roughly five miles] from the coast, and as we had never seen such a large town in the Island of Cuba nor in Hispaniola, we named it the Great Cairo."

Indian dwellings constructed from mud and reeds, found the city so impressive that they named it the Great Cairo.

On March 4, Córdoba sent his two shallower draft vessels near the shoreline for a closer look. Soon ten large dugout canoes, each carrying up to thirty Mayan Indians, approached the Spanish vessels. The Spaniards waved their capes at the natives, encouraging them to come closer. Boldly, the natives slid their dugouts alongside Córdoba's flagship and boarded her.

To prove their friendly intentions, Córdoba and his men gave the Mayans gifts of green glass beads. While these trinkets were inexpensive among the Spaniards, the Indians, who lacked the technology to manufacture them, valued them highly. Indicating peaceful intent was simple enough. More detailed communication proved difficult since neither side understood the other's language. After struggling with sign language for some time, the Spaniards concluded that the Indian cacique (chieftain) intended to return with canoes to transport the Europeans to his town the next day.

Ambush

As expected, the natives arrived on the following day with twelve large canoes. Smiling and gesturing, they shouted, *"Cones catoche,"* which the Spaniards later learned meant "Come to my houses." Because of this, the Spaniards named the location Cape Catoche, a name it still bears. Weapons in hand, Córdoba and his men allowed the Indians to transport them to the shore. The Spaniards then followed their brown-skinned hosts inland. Suddenly, at a shouted command from the cacique, Indian warriors rushed from the surrounding bushes and attacked the Spaniards. Fifteen of Córdoba's men suffered wounds almost immediately. Recovering from the initial surprise, the Spaniards opened fire with their matchlock muskets and crossbows. The Europeans' superior weaponry quickly turned the tables, and the Indians fled. The Spaniards' counterattack killed fifteen Indians and captured two.

Once the natives had fled, Córdoba and his men entered the town. Three masonry buildings, apparently used as temples, surrounded a small plaza. The Spaniards ransacked the temples, carrying off small figurines and jewelry made of gold mixed with copper. Afterward, Córdoba and his men returned to their ships with their two prisoners. The bewildered Indians soon found themselves baptized into the Catholic faith, assigned the Christian names Julian and Melchior, and forced to join their captors. Despite the wounds they suffered in the ambush, Díaz wrote that the Spaniards were optimistic. They had discovered a new land well populated by people far more sophisticated than their Cuban neighbors. More importantly, they had found gold. For the next fifteen days, Córdoba's fleet sailed west around the Yucatán Peninsula, taking care

After fooling the Spaniards with their friendly overtures, the Indians attack Córdoba's men.

to anchor well offshore at night in case the natives attempted another ambush. At last, their casks leaking and their drinking water almost exhausted, the Spaniards put ashore at Campeche to replenish their supply. With the Cape Catoche ambush in mind, they came ashore alert and prepared for battle. As they refilled their casks, natives dressed in cotton clothing approached them and by sign language asked the Spaniards if they had come from the east. According to Díaz, the Indians also may have betrayed some prior knowledge of Europeans.

> They . . . made signs with their hands to find out whether we came from the direction of the sunrise, repeating the word "Castilan" "Castilan" and we did not understand what they meant by Castilan.[3]

Since Castile was the largest of the kingdoms that comprised Spain, Spaniards often called themselves Castilians. Apparently, Díaz did not see any special meaning in the Indian usage.

Córdoba accepted the natives' invitation to visit their town, but the Spaniards met a hostile reception when they arrived. Large numbers of warriors armed with lances and bows gathered around them. As the tension mounted, the Spaniards noticed an altar heavily clotted with blood as if the Indians had recently offered sacrifices there. Priests, their bodies covered with blood, emerged from a temple and piled wood on the ground. Through sign language they warned the Spaniards that if they did not leave the land before the fire went out, the warriors would kill them all. After setting the wood ablaze, the priests walked away, leaving the Spaniards to face a howling mob of warriors. Cór-

doba and his men realized that they were outnumbered, and they reluctantly returned to their ships. Díaz described the scene in *Discovery and Conquest*:

> After ordering fire to be put to the reeds, the priests withdrew without further speech. Then the warriors who were drawn up in battle array began to whistle and sound their trumpets and drums. When we perceived their menacing appearance and saw great squadrons of Indians bearing down on us . . . fear fell on us, so we determined to retreat to the coast in good order.[4]

The fleet again set sail and made slow progress up the coast, finally putting ashore at Champoton for water. Again warriors arrived, fearsome men armed with bows, lances, slings, two-handed wood-and-stone swords, and shields, their bodies painted black, white, and red. Clearly, the entire country now knew of the white-skinned intruders and had risen in arms to meet them. Like the Indians at Campeche, the people of Champoton used sign language to ask if the Spaniards had come from the land where the sun rises. The Indians' obsession with this issue puzzled Córdoba's men. Two years would pass before they would understand the question's importance.

An Uneven Battle

Although the Spaniards understood little the Indians said, it was obvious they were potentially hostile. That night the Europeans posted guards and slept fitfully, surrounded by the sounds of massing warriors. Shortly before dawn, the soldiers held council and, seeing themselves surrounded and outnumbered two hundred to one, decided to stand and fight for their lives. A blizzard of Indian arrows fell on the Spaniards, wounding eighty of them. Díaz suffered three arrow wounds, one of which passed through his ribs.

Above the roar of battle, the soldiers could hear the Indians shouting, "*Al Calachuni!*" which they later learned meant "Let us attack the captain and kill him!"[5] The warriors' fury focused on Córdoba, who survived the battle in spite of ten wounds. By now all the Spaniards had suffered wounds, fifty were dead, and two had been captured alive. Seeing the futility of standing and fighting, the Spanish captain ordered his men to fight their way to the landing boats. Indian bravery proved no match for the conquistadors' great two-handed steel swords. The Spaniards pierced the ring of warriors, poured onto the beach, and shoved their boats into the breakers. Several of the boats had become waterlogged and began to sink, forcing their wounded passengers to swim or cling to the half-sunken craft. Jubilant warriors ran into the surf hurling lances and unleashing arrows as long as there was any hope of inflicting further damage on the white men. Seeing the little army's dilemma, the pilot of Córdoba's shallowest draft vessel sailed close to the shore to pick up the struggling survivors. In *Discovery and Conquest*, Díaz confessed his great relief at finding himself alive when the battle ended:

> Ah! then to hear the yells, hisses and cries, as the enemy showered arrows on us and hurled lances with all their might, wounding us sorely. . . . Thank God! by a great effort we escaped with our lives from the clutches of those people.[6]

Córdoba's shattered force sailed away from Champoton. The battle had lasted only an hour.

The Sad Journey Home

Within days, five Spanish soldiers died from their wounds, and their comrades tossed their bodies overboard. Some men became so weak that there were too few men to sail all three boats. The Spaniards stripped their smallest ship of its rigging and tackle, burned it, and distributed the men between the remaining two ships. Daily, the Spaniards' morale sank. Not only were half their comrades dead and the rest wounded, but they now suffered from thirst, since they had lost many water casks in the battle at Champoton. In *Discovery and Conquest*, Díaz bemoaned the suffering the Spaniards experienced:

> So great was our thirst that our mouths and tongues were cracked with dryness, and there was nothing to give us relief. Oh! what hardships one endures, when discovering new lands. . . . [N]o one can appreciate the excessive hardships who has not passed through them as we did.[7]

The survivors decided to return to Cuba.

After the weakened Spaniards had endured another violent storm, their best pilot, Antón de Alaminos, persuaded Córdoba to sail to Cuba by way of Florida. He assured them the route would be shorter and bring them to a reliable source of fresh water. Within four days the fleet reached the location where Ponce de León had landed and collected water

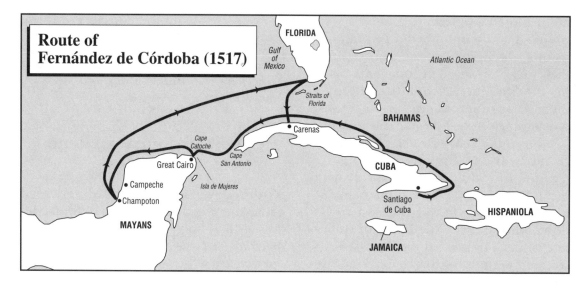

Route of Fernández de Córdoba (1517)

FLORIDA

Gulf of Mexico

Atlantic Ocean

Straits of Florida

BAHAMAS

Carenas

Cape Catoche

Cape San Antonio

Great Cairo

Isla de Mujeres

Campeche

Champoton

CUBA

Santiago de Cuba

HISPANIOLA

MAYANS

JAMAICA

during his search for the legendary fountain of youth. Córdoba, by now dying of his wounds and dehydration, assembled a landing party from the men who had most fully recovered from their wounds and ordered them not to return without full water casks. Alaminos, who had sailed with Ponce de León, warned the men who were going ashore to expect hostile Indians. Once ashore, the Spaniards dug wells and found abundant water, but as Alaminos had warned, Indian warriors arrived in force and drove them back to their boats. Only superior weaponry and fighting skill allowed the conquistadors to escape with their water casks.

Refreshed by the water, Córdoba and his men sailed their battered ships back to Cuba, anchoring where Havana now stands. Within days, Córdoba died of his wounds. He had lost one ship, half his command, and all of his men were wounded, but they had discovered a new land. News of this new land and its warlike people spread quickly throughout Cuba. Governor Velázquez was particularly interested in the news of gold and great cities. He soon assembled a fleet to return to Yucatán. Several of Córdoba's battle-scarred veterans, who had just survived the most terrifying experience of their young lives, would sail with it.

Chapter

2 The Grijalva Expedition

From a distance of almost five hundred years, the Córdoba expedition seems a disaster. To the Spaniards in Cuba in 1517, hardship and death were just the costs of doing business in the New World. Certainly Diego Velázquez did not grieve long over the casualties from Córdoba's mainland misadventure. The governor found the reports of gold and advanced civilizations so tantalizing that he refitted two of Córdoba's ships, bought two more, and purchased weapons and trade goods for the return trip to Yucatán.

Velázquez entrusted command of the expedition to his nephew, Juan de Grijalva. He also appointed three prominent *encomenderos* (men who held grants of land and Indian laborers), Alonso de Ávila, Pedro de Alvarado, and Francisco de Montejo, to command three ships in the fleet on the condition that they provision the vessels at their own expense. Grijalva and his lieutenants had no problem recruiting fighting men and sailors. News of the bountiful land to the west had spread rapidly among Cuba's landless adventurers, and 240 quickly volunteered.

On April 8, 1518, Grijalva set sail for Yucatán, intending to retrace Córdoba's route, but unpredictable winds and currents made navigation more of an art than a science in the sixteenth century. After

Juan de Grijalva commanded a renewed effort to obtain the riches of the New World after the failed Córdoba expedition.

eighteen days at sea, Grijalva's fleet dropped anchor at the island of Cozumel. The Spaniards went ashore and entered a town on the island only to find all the Indians had fled at their approach. As the Spaniards surveyed the abandoned town, an attractive Indian woman approached them and, much to their surprise, they understood her.

The Spirit of the Conquistador

Bernal Díaz and several other Spaniards accompanied three expeditions to Yucatán even though they suffered repeated wounds and knew they risked death. In this excerpt from Conquest of Mexico, *nineteenth-century historian William H. Prescott explores their motivation.*

"It is difficult for those of our time . . . to picture . . . the feelings of the men who lived in the sixteenth century. The dread mystery, which had so long hung over the great deep, had been removed . . . when Columbus launched his bold bark on its dark and unknown waters. . . .

The career thus thrown open had all the fascinations of a desperate hazard, on which the adventurer staked all his hope of fortune, fame, and life itself. It was not often . . . that he won the rich prize which he most coveted; but then he was sure to win . . . glory, scarcely less dear to his chivalrous spirit; and, if he survived to return to his home, he had wonderful stories to recount, of perilous chances among the strange people he had visited. . . . These reports added fresh fuel to imaginations already warmed by the study of those tales of chivalry which formed the favourite reading of the Spaniards of that period. . . . Romance and reality acted on each other, and the soul of the Spaniard was exalted to that pitch of enthusiasm, which enabled him to encounter the terrible trials that lay in the path of the discoverer. . . . The life of the cavalier of that day was romance put into action."

Using the language of the Jamaican Indians, she explained that she and ten other Indians, including her husband, had set out from Jamaica on a fishing expedition two years before. Strong currents, however, had forced them to Cozumel. The islanders had captured them and sacrificed all but her to idols. The Jamaican woman viewed the Spaniards as liberators and willingly accompanied them. Grijalva sent her to invite the hiding islanders to meet with the Spaniards, but they refused. After waiting a few profitless days, Grijalva weighed anchor and turned his ships toward Yucatán.

A Battle At Champoton

The Spaniards made landfall at Champoton, where the Indians had soundly defeated Córdoba's men the previous year. Sighting the Spanish ships, the warriors of Champoton armed themselves, lined the shore, and taunted the European intruders, daring them to do battle. Grijalva had expected opposition and loaded half his heavily armed soldiers into landing boats and sent them toward the beach. As the boats neared the shore, the Indians showered the Spaniards with arrows and javelins, wounding many. Unlike Córdoba's men, Grijalva's soldiers knew what to expect at Champoton and came prepared. Pressing on through the storm of wooden missiles, they dragged their boats onto the beach, unsheathed their swords, and deployed several falconets (small cannon) that they had brought ashore.

Now the warriors of Champoton faced the Spaniards' long Toledo blades and deadly fire from crossbows, matchlock muskets, and cannon. To their credit, they did not run when faced with these fearsome weapons from another world, but they could not hold their ground. Slowly, the natives retreated into the swamps, fighting as they went. Swarms of locusts rose from the battlefield, distracting the Europeans. Since in the thick of the fighting the soldiers often mistook incoming arrows for locusts, they sometimes failed to raise their shields in time to avoid injury. The Spaniards took possession of the town but at the cost of seven dead. Grijalva suffered three arrow wounds.

For three days the Spaniards explored the area and took soundings of the waters. They also hunted the deer and rabbits that abounded around Champoton, enjoying a welcome change from their usual shipboard diet of salt pork and cassava bread. Grijalva's men had taken several Indian prisoners during the fighting. Now, through Julian and Melchior, the Spaniards assured the captives that they would rather trade than fight. Giving the prisoners some glass beads, they sent them to persuade their caciques to return to the town for a conference. Neither the prisoners nor the caciques returned, causing Grijalva to suspect Julian and Melchior had not faithfully translated his message.

The People of Tabasco

Again failing to find willing trading partners among the Indians, Grijalva led his fleet westward along the coast. The fleet passed the Rio de Tabasco (which the Spaniards renamed Rio de Grijalva), and Grijalva sent his soldiers on the two shallowest draft ships upstream to explore the land. As the Spaniards sailed inland, the sounds of axes felling trees for fortifications rang out across the water. It seemed the entire country had risen in arms against the Europeans. When Grijalva sent his soldiers ashore, fifty Indian canoes filled with warriors moved in to attack.

The Spaniards acted quickly. Through Julian and Melchior they called to the Indians, insisting that they came in peace. The main body of warriors paused, and thirty of them advanced and held council with Grijalva and his men. The Spaniards gave the Indians the usual gifts of glass beads and urged them to trade. Their king, Charles I, they added, was very powerful and the natives should accept him as their new ruler. The Indians dismissed the idea of swearing loyalty to this unknown king but found the beads, which they considered gems, impressive. The Indians agreed to consult their chiefs and decide whether to make war or have peace. Should the decision favor war, they warned, the Spaniards would not only find the men of Tabasco far more formidable as warriors than the men of Champoton, but they would face a native army twenty-four thousand strong. Despite these ominous words, Grijalva and his men remained ashore to await the Tabascans' decision.

The following day, thirty Indians arrived with gifts of food and with trade goods, including cotton cloth, jewelry, and sculptures of gold. While the golden objects were often mixed with copper and consequently of modest value, the Spaniards were delighted to learn that the yellow metal was found in Yucatán. The Indians willingly traded their goods for Spanish trinkets, so the Spaniards asked if they had more gold. No, they answered, but there was plenty more to the west. Pointing inland they said "Colua" and "Mexico."

Realizing their fleet lay in an unprotected anchorage and fearing it could be struck by a northerly gale, the Spaniards decided to leave Tabasco and sail farther west. Besides, that would carry the conquistadors toward the land where gold was to be found. After two days sailing close to the coast, the Spaniards encountered Indian warriors marching along the shore, shouting taunts and insults at them. Each warrior carried a tortoiseshell shield that glittered in the sunlight, convincing some of the treasure-hungry adventurers that the Indians made their weapons of gold.

Grijalva Meets the Aztecs

As Grijalva's men sailed in search of riches, the men who possessed those riches searched for the Spaniards. Instead of seeing the usual masses of hostile natives challenging them from the shores, the conquistadors now saw large numbers of Indians waving white banners and beckoning peacefully to them. Realizing this could be a trap, Grijalva dispatched a small detachment to determine the Indians' identity and intentions. They soon learned that these were not Mayans, the people they had encountered up to then.

These men came in the name of the great Aztec king, Montezuma.

Montezuma's spies had already told him of the men who sailed on white wings from the direction of the sunrise. The king knew that this handful of white men had defeated many times their numbers at Champoton. Pictures painted on cotton cloth and carried by native runners hundreds of miles to the Aztec capital depicted bearded men with shining skins and fiery weapons (armor and guns). Montezuma had learned all he could from rumors and observation at a distance. Now his representatives would speak to these beings whose ships had touched his domain.

In his account of the conquest, Díaz admitted he and his comrades found this

Montezuma, ruler of the Aztecs. Aztec spies stationed throughout the empire detected Grijalva's arrival almost immediately.

An ancient Aztec drawing depicts the ritual sacrifice of members of enemy tribes.

friendly reception amazing. Not until later did he understand that the Aztecs' behavior grew out of the fear that the Spaniards might be more than men. In *The Discovery and Conquest of Mexico*, Díaz explained the Aztecs' behavior.

> It is a fact, as we now know, that their Indian ancestors had foretold that men with beards would come from the direction of the sunrise and would rule over them. Whatever the reason may have been many Indians sent by the Great Montezuma were watching for us . . . with long poles, and on every pole a banner of white cotton cloth, which they waved and called to us, as though making signals of peace, to come to them.[8]

Montezuma's representatives treated the Spaniards with every courtesy. They gave the Europeans gifts of food, including turkeys, fruit, and bread, and burned incense to honor the white-skinned strangers. More importantly to the Spaniards, the Indians willingly exchanged golden objects, cloth, and featherwork for Spanish trinkets. Despite the fact that the Spaniards did not understand the Aztec language, they communicated through signs and after three days had acquired a valuable cargo in native goods.

The Island of Sacrifice

Once the natives stopped bringing gold to the Spaniards, Grijalva sailed farther west along the coast. As the fleet passed some of the larger coastal islands, the Spanish commander noted some roads and saw smoke rising through the trees. A landing party disembarked to investigate and found stone houses and temples. To their horror, they discovered the remains of five dismembered human bodies in front of the temples. Revolted by the sight, the Spaniards sailed away from the island and marked it on their charts as the Island of Sacrifice.

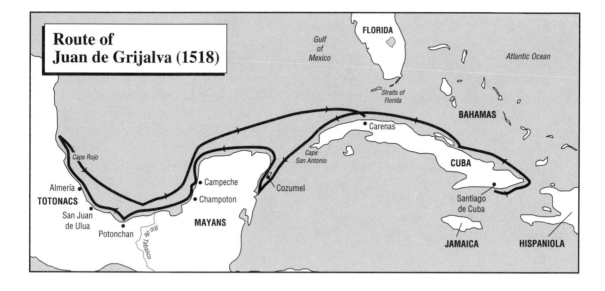

Despite this grisly evidence of the natives' habits, the Spaniards continued to explore the coastline and attempt trade with the local inhabitants. For seven days they camped among the sand dunes near the present site of Veracruz. Here mosquitoes swarmed them day and night, and the hardships of the voyage began to take their toll. Bread supplies had become black with mold and alive with weevils. Thirteen of their soldiers died of wounds. Still the Spaniards remained because Montezuma's agents arrived and sold them a few small golden objects.

Torn between returning with their treasure to the safety of Cuba and seeking more gold in the new land while their condition worsened, the soldiers compromised. Pedro de Alvarado sailed with the best ship and much of the treasure to Cuba. Once there he could give Governor Velázquez a report of the expedition's progress and seek reinforcements for the little army. In the meantime, Grijalva followed the coast in its northward curve, passing by many sizable towns.

While the fleet was anchored at the mouth of the Rio de Canoas near one of these towns, the conquistadors allowed themselves to be caught off guard by hostile Indians. With little warning, Indian canoes suddenly surrounded the Spanish vessels. Some of the natives pressed the attack so fiercely that they pulled alongside one Spanish ship and cut the anchor cable with copper axes. Only with help from the two remaining vessels did the Spaniards escape.

After the battle at Rio de Canoas, Grijalva sailed north until his fleet was forced to retrace its path by powerful currents. Along the way they found Indians willing to trade some low-grade golden objects near Coatzacoalcos. While the Spaniards had become accustomed to seeing the modest little sculptures, their imaginations soared when the Indians offered them what appeared to be six hundred highly polished, beautifully crafted golden axes. Convinced they had finally found the golden treasure they had sought, the soldiers bought them all, only to learn later that they were not gold at all. In his account of the conquest, Díaz sheepishly admitted that each side had taken advantage of the other.

We were very well contented thinking that they were made of debased [mixed with other metals] gold, and the Indians were even more contented with their beads, but it was no good for either party, for the axes were made of copper and the beads were valueless.[9]

To Cuba with a Golden Cargo

Forty-five days after sailing from Yucatán, Grijalva's fleet returned to Santiago, Cuba. Alvarado's report to Velázquez and news of the treasure his ship carried had spread throughout the island. Anxious to exploit the opportunity for conquest and wealth, the governor and several investors were already outfitting a much larger fleet to return to Yucatán, but he had not chosen Grijalva to command it. The decision surprised Grijalva. Compared to the Córdoba expedition, his journey had enjoyed much greater success. Not only had he returned from Yucatán with his fleet intact, he had traded profitably with the natives.

Nevertheless, Velázquez was dissatisfied with the results. While the governor lacked authorization from the Spanish government to found a colony, and while he had not instructed Grijalva to do so, he feared other Spanish governors in the Caribbean and the Gulf of Mexico would claim Yucatán before he could. Grijalva, like a good soldier, had followed his instructions to trade, resisted his soldiers' suggestions that they use their meager resources to plant a town, and returned with

---

The Island of Sacrifice

The Spaniards found the Indian custom of human sacrifice, a practice long abhorred in the Christian, Jewish, and Moslem worlds, disgusting. In The Discovery and Conquest of Mexico, *Díaz described the scene on the Island of Sacrifice.*

"As soon as the boats were launched the Captain Juan de Grijalva and many of us soldiers went off to visit the Island for we saw smoke rising from it, and we found two masonry houses very well built, each house with steps leading up to some altars, and on these altars were idols with evil looking bodies, and that chests [of human sacrificial victims] had been cut open, and the arms and thighs had been cut off and the walls were covered with blood.

At all this we stood greatly amazed, and gave the Island the name of the Isla de Sacrificios [Island of Sacrifice] and it is so marked on the charts."

a profit. In his account of the conquest, Díaz claimed Velázquez and Grijalva's men were pleased with the expedition's accomplishments.

> When the Governor saw the gold that we brought . . . which . . . amounted in all to twenty thousand dollars, he was well contented. . . . Most of us soldiers who were there said we should prefer to go again under Juan de Grijalva, for he was a good captain, and there was no fault to be found either with his person or his capacity for command.[10]

However, Gómara, in his biography of Cortés, said Velázquez was angry because Grijalva had not colonized the new land.

> If he had been aware of his good fortune he would have planted a colony in that land, as his companions begged him to do. . . . But this great good was not for one who could not recognize it, although he excused himself by saying that he had not gone there to found a colony, but to trade and discover whether the land of Yucatán was an island or not. He gave it up also because of his fear of the many people and the great size of the country. . . .

> When he arrived [in Cuba] Diego Velázquez refused to see him—a fate that he deserved.[11]

Whatever Velázquez's true feelings may have been, one thing was clear: The commander of the next fleet would not hesitate to colonize. And he would not rest until he had seized the source of the Indians' gold.

3 "I Came to Get Gold!"

Some people change the world by sheer determination and force of will. Velázquez's choice to lead the third Spanish expedition to Yucatán, Hernando Cortés, was such a man. Like so many of Spain's greatest conquistadors, he came from Estremadura, a region of high plains, where tough men and women forced a living out of arid, unyielding land by herding livestock. Here boys grew to manhood amid stories of the *reconquista,* the reconquest of Spain from the Moors (Moslems) by Christian warriors.

The wars to rid Spain of the Moors had raged off and on for seven hundred years. In the late fifteenth century, Spain's dual monarchs, Ferdinand and Isabella, conquered the last of the Moorish-held territories in Spain. With the formal surrender of Granada in 1492, Spain was unified. So it was that in 1502, Queen Isabella expelled hundreds of thousands of Moors, making Spain more Catholic and making more land available for distribution. According to historian Wallace K. Ferguson, Spain's nobles had become a warlike and independent lot.

The nobles and the crusading orders who spearheaded the reconquest were rewarded with huge grants of land, over which . . . they acquired sovereign powers. Bred in a tradition of perpetual guerrilla warfare, the nobles also fought one another and their kings as fiercely as they fought the Moor.[12]

His own missionary zeal as well as the promise of fame and fortune drove Hernando Cortés to command an expedition to the New World.

Cortés

Born in 1485, Hernando Cortés was too young to help drive the Moslems from his homeland, but Spain's fighting men found new pagans (non-Christians) to convert and new lands to possess in the world Christopher Columbus had discovered. Like many of these men, Cortés came from a family with a respected name and little wealth. At his parents' insistence he began studying law in Salamanca at age fourteen, hoping to undertake a respectable career in government service. After two years, he tired of his books and wandered Spain in search of romance and adventure. There were few indications of Cortés's greatness during these years. He lived a life without clear goals and developed a reputation as a woman chaser, even dallying at times with married women. On one occasion he fell from a garden wall as he attempted to secretly enter his married mistress's house. As he lay stunned by the fall, he found his mistress's

---

The Character of Hernando Cortés

Surrounded by controversy for more than four centuries, Hernando Cortés remains a commanding figure in both Spanish and Mexican history. In his introduction to William Weber Johnson's Cortés, *J. H. Plumb sketches Cortés's character.*

"Only Spain in the sixteenth century could have bred Cortés—poor yet arrogant, chivalrous yet cruel, pious yet sinful, generous yet full of greed; above all, a man of decisive action, but capable of patience and guile, a man who belonged to a world that had passed yet who launched half a continent and its people into the mainstream of history. . . . Unbelievable success came to Cortés: with a handful of men and a few horses he toppled the greatest, the most warlike of all American empires—the Aztecs of Mexico. . . .

It is impossible to understand the triumph of Cortés and his captains if one ignores the depth and sincerity of their religious beliefs, no matter how brutal and sensual they might be in action. They could torture, kill and rape, but they knew how to pray to the Virgin and the saints. . . .

The whole of the great Spanish empire was a curious mixture of crusading zeal and heartless greed. Cortés was full of lust—for women, for riches, for power. Nevertheless he was deeply pious, certain of Heaven, careless about death, hence capable of a daring that still amazes."

The island of Hispaniola under attack by Spanish conquistadors. Cortés would visit Hispaniola in 1504.

husband poised above him with his sword drawn. Facing certain death, he was spared when the offended husband's mother-in-law pleaded for his life.

However, even then he was developing traits that would serve him well during the conquest. He was handy with a sword and an excellent horseman. He was clever and blessed with a generous spirit and a ready wit. He had a gift for both the written and spoken word and could be cunningly persuasive. Despite his moral weaknesses, he was fiercely devoted to the Catholic Church. Perhaps just as importantly, the restless, unfocused boy was maturing into an ambitious, energetic man. Clearly, a young Spanish gentleman's best prospects for advancement, glory, and wealth lay in the New World, a world the Spaniards still

believed lay on Asia's eastern edge. In 1504 Cortés, with his parents' blessing and financial help, booked passage on a ship bound for Hispaniola. Upon reaching the island, Cortés petitioned the governor's office for a grant of land with, he emphasized, substantial gold deposits. From the beginning he made it clear that he intended to grow rich quickly through mining and had no desire to demean himself by farming. In his classic account of the conquest, William Prescott tells of the impatient teenager's demand for instant riches.

> Immediately on landing, Cortés repaired [went] to the house of the governor [Nicolás de Ovando], to whom he had been personally known in Spain. Ovando was absent . . . but the

young man was kindly received by the secretary, who assured him there would be no doubt of his obtaining a liberal grant of land to settle on. "But I came to get gold," replied Cortés, "not to till the soil like a peasant."[13]

Although Hispaniola's mines produced a steady trickle of gold, the amounts remained small compared to Spain's later colonial possessions. Eventually, Governor Ovando persuaded Cortés that a grant of land and Indian laborers would provide him a slower but more certain path to riches.

For seven years, Cortés developed his Hispaniolan estate, selling salt pork and other supplies to seagoing vessels, but he still hungered for greater wealth. In 1511 he accompanied Diego Velázquez on an expedition to conquer Cuba. As Velázquez's clerk and treasurer, Cortés kept records of the amount of loot seized by the army and saw to it that the king's share, the "King's Fifth," was properly set aside. The conquest of Cuba with its peaceful natives proved relatively easy. More importantly for Cortés, the campaign brought him to the attention of Velázquez, who was impressed both with his fighting ability and his administrative skills.

Now governor of Cuba, Velázquez granted Cortés a sizable allotment of land and Indians at Santiago de Baracoa, the first Spanish town on the island. Drawing on his Hispaniolan experience, Cortés quickly undertook a profitable trade selling his estate's produce. He imported European crops, became the first Spaniard to introduce cattle to the island, and raised horses—priceless animals due to their scarcity in the West Indies (the is-

lands of the Caribbean). Cortés also found the gold mines on his land far more lucrative than those on Hispaniola. Now a gentleman of substance, he courted the pretty Catalina Xuarez, whose father had brought his daughters to Cuba in search of rich husbands. In a moment of weakness, Cortés proposed marriage to her and later changed his mind. By this time Velázquez, who was a friend of the Xuarez family, learned of Cortés's faithlessness, insisted the unwilling suitor make good his promise, and put him in irons until he had a change of heart. Cortés, already angered by the governor's failure to grant him a larger estate, refused to comply, and twice escaped from his imprisonment. Eventually, Cortés relented, reconciled with Velázquez, and wed the fair Catalina. For his part, Velázquez unwisely concluded he had his headstrong young lieutenant firmly under control.

Velázquez Appoints Cortés Captain-General

Catalina must have found Cortés an excellent match. He supported her in lavish style, buying her expensive clothes and entertaining guests on a scale even a well-to-do landholder could not long sustain. It became common knowledge among the Spanish settlers that Cortés's ambition had, as usual, outgrown his income. Now, as his hunger for wealth grew, news of Grijalva's golden cargo from Yucatán and of Velázquez's search for a new expedition commander again drew his attention eastward. Discreetly, he persuaded Andrés de Duero, a merchant close to Velázquez, and Amador de Lares, the king's accountant, to convince the governor to appoint him to command the new Yucatán expedition. In return for this, he assured them, they would divide the profits from the enterprise. According to Bernal Díaz, Duero and Lares tirelessly campaigned for Cortés.

Duero and the accountant went to work on Diego Velázquez. They addressed him in honeyed words, praising Cortés highly as the very man for the post of Captain, since he was not only enterprising but knew how to command and inspire fear. Moreover, they said he would carry out whatever orders he was given. . . . They also pointed out that since Velázquez had been his sponsor in marriage to Doña Catalina Suarez [Xuarez], he was in fact the Governor's stepson. Thus they persuaded Velázquez to choose Cortés as Captain-General.[14]

Whether or not Duero and Lares effectively carried out their end of the bargain, Cortés's qualifications made him an attractive choice for Velázquez. Velázquez

---

Spain Conquers the West Indies

Unlike the people of Middle America, the people of Hispaniola and Cuba were docile and easily conquered by the Spaniards. In this excerpt from Cortés and Montezuma, *Maurice Collis notes the West Indians' tragic fate.*

"[In the early sixteenth century] the Spaniards had been organizing their first discovery, the West Indies. The island of Hispaniola or Little Spain was the first to be settled. Adventurers of all classes sailed across the Atlantic, hoping to get rich quick. Some were granted estates and labour to work them. The labourers were the unfortunate inhabitants, who before the arrival of the Spaniards had been living a carefree life under their chiefs. They were amiable, happy peoples, rather like South Sea Islanders. Reduced to the condition of serfs [servants forced to work on the estates of nobles], made to work hard on the plantations and at washing for gold, and very cruelly treated besides, they lost heart and died in great numbers.

Among the adventurers who came out was Hernan Cortés . . . [who] arrived in Hispaniola in 1504, aged nineteen. . . . In 1511, at the age of twenty-six, he joined the expedition of Diego Velázquez . . . to subdue the great neighbouring island of Cuba. . . . The conquest was easy, as the inhabitants were too terrified of the Spaniards to make a stubborn resistance."

needed something of a rascal to command the expedition, someone willing to break the rules when the occasion demanded. Because of Grijalva's devotion to legality and his timidity, the governor had already lost valuable time in the race to colonize Yucatán. The new commander would have to stretch Velázquez's written instructions to trade with the natives and establish a colony even though the governor could not authorize him to do so. Velázquez also needed someone who would willingly gamble his life and his fortune to conquer a new land. In the years since he had conquered Cuba, Velázquez had grown fat, prosperous, and content to let younger, more nimble men take the risks.

"A Rogue on a Leash"

In every respect, Cortés met the qualifications. Impatient with rules, he seldom failed to seize an opportunity. Impetuous and creative, he was already campaigning for a chance to risk all he had for the chance to gain more. While he had amassed enough wealth to share the expedition's expense, his extravagant lifestyle drove him to find new sources of income. A veteran of the Indian wars in Hispaniola and Velázquez's own campaigns in Cuba, he possessed the administrative and military skills the job demanded. For all this, Duero and Lares persuaded the governor that Cortés as captain-general of the expedition would remain loyal and obedient, conquer this distant land in Velázquez's name, and divide the spoils with both governor and king. If Cortés was a rogue, Velázquez intended that he be a rogue on a leash.

Velázquez's decision to appoint Cortés captain-general of the expedition sparked some resentment among a number of Spanish *hidalgos* (nobles) who had sought the position. Despite the risks involved, this newest expedition to the golden land had fired the islanders' imaginations and whetted their appetites for glory and profit. Not surprisingly, many of Velázquez's relatives considered themselves more deserving of the appointment and tried to reverse his decision. Just as Duero and Lares had bombarded the governor with Cortés's praise, Velázquez's kinsmen reminded him of his new captain-general's ambition and independent ways. As Cortés and Duero accompanied Velázquez to mass one day, an eccentric known to the Spaniards as the Mad Cervantes scampered around the governor, taunting and warning that Cortés would betray him. "Take care, Don Diego, or he may run off with your fleet!" he cried. Convinced Velázquez's kinsmen had arranged the incident, Duero slapped the fool and commanded him to be silent. According to Bernal Díaz, the Mad Cervantes ignored Duero's blows and shouted more loudly:

> Long live Don Diego . . . and his bold Captain! And let me tell you, friend Diego, I would rather go off with him to these new rich lands than stay behind and watch you weeping over the bad bargain you've made today.[15]

The warning may have planted doubt in Velázquez's mind. Díaz considered the incident prophetic. "All that he said came true," he wrote in *Conquest*, "as they say the utterances of fools sometimes do."[16]

Cortés's diligence in outfitting his fleet doubtless pleased Velázquez. Velázquez invested some of his own money in the expe-

Diego Velázquez conquered Cuba and governed the island for Spain. He organized and funded other expeditions to the New World, including the one Cortés commanded.

Cortés's reliability growing, Velázquez planted several of his relatives among the volunteers, the better to keep an eye on him in a distant land.

Cortés was already keeping an eye on Velázquez. Well aware that the governor might revoke his commission, Cortés hastened his preparations. His anxiety growing by the day, Velázquez offered to buy Cortés's interest in the fleet and to replace him as captain-general, but Cortés declined the offer and reminded Velázquez that the enterprise would make them both wealthy. In November 1518 Cortés's fleet set sail from Santiago. According to the practice of the times, the fleet headed west along the Cuban coast, stopping first in Trinidad to collect supplies and recruit more men before crossing the Gulf of Mexico.

Fear of Mutiny

By this time Velázquez had learned of Cortés's dealings with Duero and Lares and feared his captain-general would mutiny at the first opportunity. The governor rushed orders to Trinidad's *alcalde* (mayor), Francisco Verdugo, to arrest Cortés and detain the fleet. Learning of the orders, Cortés smoothly persuaded Verdugo's lieutenants it was unnecessary to carry them out. Then he sent one of his subordinates, Diego de Ordaz, to deal with Verdugo. Ordaz assured the *alcalde* that the captain-general remained loyal to Velázquez and that the governor's orders served no useful purpose. Besides, he added ominously, Cortés commanded a large armed force and had become immensely popular in Cuba while assembling the expedition. Any attempt to arrest him might spark insurrection. Thus

dition, but the new captain-general poured his fortune into buying supplies and equipment, including crossbows, muskets, cannon, powder, shot, and several of the island's precious horses. As he exhausted his own funds, he borrowed still more, using his estate as collateral for the loan. No one could doubt Cortés's commitment to the enterprise. If Yucatán did not yield the riches of which he had dreamed, he would be ruined financially. Ever a good salesman, Cortés spoke confidently of the expedition's prospects and made himself the image of prosperity, dressing in a plumed hat, velvet cloak, and gold jewelry. He issued a proclamation inviting the brave Spanish warriors of Cuba to join him in the quest for Yucatán's gold, and 350 men flocked to his standard. His doubts about

Cortés's fleet sails to the New World. Almost as soon as Velázquez appointed Cortés to head the expedition, he had second thoughts about Cortés's loyalty.

warned, Verdugo allowed Cortés to continue provisioning at Trinidad unmolested for ten days.

The process repeated itself when Cortés's fleet reached Havana. Again Velázquez sent orders that no one obeyed. Some of his subordinates decided to ignore his commands because they felt they had been slighted in grants of land and Indians. Some fell prey to Cortés's persuasive powers. Now momentarily beyond Velázquez's

power, Cortés completed his provisioning and sent the governor one last letter announcing his intention to sail for Yucatán. On February 10, 1519, the fleet sailed west from Cuba. Boasting eleven ships, fourteen cannon, and 508 men, including musketeers and crossbowmen, it was the most formidable Spanish armament ever to penetrate Yucatán. It would challenge the greatest empire in the Americas, an empire that commanded millions.

4 The Return to Yucatán

It took a determined man to keep an army of conquistadors in hand. Greedy, quick-tempered, independent, and defensive of their personal honor, they gave neither their loyalty nor their obedience easily. Now with his fleet at the western edge of the known world, Cortés lost no time in taking command of his men. He ordered the fleet to rendezvous before sailing to Cozumel, but Pedro de Alvarado's pilot ignored the captain-general's command and arrived at the island two days ahead of the rest. Terrified by the sight of the strange Spanish vessels, most of the Indians fled their town. Always impetuous, Alvarado landed his men, captured three Indians, foraged for food, and looted the natives' homes and temples.

In the meantime, a storm had scattered the other ships in the fleet on the crossing from Cuba to Yucatán. A rudder broke on one of the ships, and supervising the repairs delayed Cortés even longer. When he reached Cozumel and learned what had happened, Cortés immediately put Alvarado's pilot in chains for his disobedience. He then scolded Alvarado for mistreating the Indians, telling his hotheaded lieutenant that the Spaniards would never gain control of the country if his men stole the natives' possessions. Using Melchior as an interpreter, he assured the captives of his peaceful intentions, gave them gifts of beads and shirts, and returned the stolen items. Then he told them to bring their caciques to meet with him, and set them free.

The next day, the chiefs and their people returned to the town. Cortés ordered his men to treat them well, and relations between the two peoples proceeded smoothly. To the amazement of Córdoba's

In hopes of getting a jump on his commander, Pedro de Alvarado (pictured) sped ahead to Cozumel, allowing his men to loot Indian settlements.

and Grijalva's veterans, some of the islanders acted as servants for the Spaniards, and others supplied them abundantly with food. This preferential treatment may have had little to do with Cortés, however. It is possible that the Mayans had long ago designated Cozumel a neutral area where warring peoples traded and worshiped in peace. Cortés and his men may have stumbled across one of the few places that the natives would receive them peacefully and the weary Spaniards could rest before touching the mainland. In the midst of gleaming white beaches washed by the crystal blue sea, on Cortés's orders the conquistadors repaired, cleaned, inspected, and practiced with their weapons. Well aware of the hostile legions Córdova and Grijalva had encountered, the captain-general prepared his men for battle, despite the islanders' friendly temperament.

Since the natives seemed cooperative and he had been told the people of Campeche had shouted "Castilan!" during the Grijalva expedition, Cortés asked the caciques if there were other white men in the area. Indeed, the chiefs gestured toward Yucatán, indicating there were other bearded men several days' march inland. On the strength of this information, Cortés asked the chiefs to locate the whites, ransom them from their Indian captors, and bring them to Cozumel. At first, the chiefs resisted, saying the warlike mainland people would surely kill and eat any messengers. Determined to learn whether any of his countrymen were captives, Cortés gave gifts to several Indians who reluctantly agreed to search for the white men. One of the Indians concealed in his long black hair a letter from the captain-general to the whites. Then, given

beads with which to ransom the Europeans, the messengers sailed for Yucatán on a brig commanded by one of Cortés's captains, Juan de Escalante.

Shortly after the brig reached Yucatán, the Indian messengers returned with the news that two white men were alive in the interior and would come join the Spaniards. For seven days, Escalante and his men waited, but the Europeans did not arrive. Finally, convinced that they were not coming, Escalante sailed for Cozumel and reported to Cortés. Escalante's failure to retrieve the mysterious Europeans disappointed the captain-general, who now returned to his primary mission, the exploration of Yucatán. Cortés ordered the fleet to sea, but not long after sailing one of the ships began leaking dangerously, forcing the entire fleet to return to Cozumel while it was repaired.

Aguilar

One day as the repairs proceeded, four men paddled ashore and beached their canoe near the Spaniards. Three fled when they saw the conquistadors, but one walked toward them. Due to his long dark hair, brown skin, and ragged loincloth, the Spaniards assumed he was an Indian until he called to them in halting Spanish. In his biography of Cortés, Francisco López de Gómara tells of the meeting. The man said in Spanish:

"Gentlemen, are you Christians?" They replied that they were Spaniards, and he was so overwhelmed at their words that he burst into tears. He asked if it was Wednesday, for he was accustomed to devoting several hours to prayer on that day. . . . Then, with tears in his eyes, he offered up a prayer to God, giving Him infinite thanks for His mercy in liberating him from those infidels and hellish men, and for restoring him to the Christians and men of his nation.[17]

The Spaniards embraced their lost countryman and led him and his Indian companions to Cortés.

The ragged man told the captain-general that he was Jerónimo de Aguilar. He and seventeen other Spaniards had been shipwrecked on Yucatán's coast and captured by the Mayans eight years before. Their captors had worked the two women in the group to death and had sacrificed most of the rest to idols and eaten their remains. For a time, the Mayans had caged and fattened Aguilar for sacrifice, but he had escaped to a kinder cacique, whom he served until Cortés ransomed him. One other survivor, having taken a Mayan wife and adopted Indian ways, chose to remain in Yucatán living as an Indian.

Cortés immediately recognized that Aguilar would be a trustworthy interpreter. Since he had been captured, Melchior had learned some Spanish, but the conquistadors always assumed he would attempt to escape. With a little practice, Aguilar would regain full command of his native tongue, and his long captivity gave him mastery of the Mayan language. His knowledge of the Yucatán natives' customs might prove invaluable. Later, Cortés, in a letter to King Charles I and his mother,

Aguilar Warns the Conquistadors of Danger in Yucatán

As they prepared to explore Yucatán, the conquistadors heard disturbing news of natives' sacrificing and devouring humans. In Cortés: The Life of the Conqueror, *Gómara quoted Jerónimo de Aguilar's tale of shipwreck and Indian cannibalism.*

"We had got as far as Jamaica when the caravel struck on the shoals . . . and twenty of us barely escaped in the ship's boat, without sails, without water, without bread, and with only one miserable pair of oars. We drifted in this fashion for thirteen or fourteen days, when we were caught in the current that runs very fast and strong to the west, and were cast ashore in a province called Maya. Seven of us had died. . . . A rascally cacique, into whose power we had fallen, sacrificed Valdivia [one of Aguilar's companions] and four others to his idols, and then ate them, making a fiesta of it and offering a share to his friends. I and six others were placed in cages to be fattened for the next banquet, and to avoid such an abominable death we broke out of our prison and fled to the woods."

Doña Juana, claimed God had delayed the fleet's departure from Cozumel so Aguilar could join them.

> We held that sudden bad weather which came upon us a great miracle and divine mystery, whereby we have come to believe that nothing can be undertaken in Your Majesties' service which does not end in good.[18]

Aguilar's account of his captivity also helped Cortés understand the gentle islanders' reluctance to undertake the mission to Yucatán. Anyone setting foot on the peninsula might die at the hands of a native warrior or under a Mayan priest's knife. Cortés provided Aguilar with clothing, welcomed him to the expedition, and readied his fleet to sail for the mainland.

The Spaniards Convert the Indians

Before his departure, Cortés met with the caciques of Cozumel at the foot of one of their temples. The Spaniards had noticed when they reached the island that in addition to their temples and altars, the natives worshiped at several large crosses. By now they also knew that the natives some-

---

The People of Cozumel Accept Catholicism

Writing King Charles I, the council of Villa Rica claimed the natives of Cozumel willingly became Catholics and Spanish subjects. This excerpt from Hernán Cortés: Letters from Mexico, *translated by A. R. Pagden, portrays this dramatic change of loyalties as a peaceful process.*

"[Cortés told the natives] that he had not come to do them harm, but to persuade them to the knowledge of our Holy Faith; and they should know that we were subjects of the most powerful monarchs [Charles I and his mother, Doña Juana] in the world, whom most of the world obeyed. What he required of them was only that the chieftains and people of the island should also owe obedience to Your Highnesses; and told them that by doing so they would be much favored, and no one thereafter would molest them. The chieftain replied that he was happy to do so and sent for all the other chieftains of the island who, when they arrived expressed satisfaction with all that Hernando Cortés had told their lord. He then commanded them to return, and so reassured them that within a few days the villages were as full of people as before, and the Indians went among us with so little fear that it seemed as if they had known us for a long time."

Under the watchful eye of a priest, Spanish conquistadors destroy Aztec idols. The Spaniards believed they had a religious duty to convert the natives to Catholicism.

times sacrificed humans on their altars. Centuries of fighting the Moors made converting nonbelievers to Christianity second nature to the conquistadors. Now confident that Aguilar could translate effectively, the captain-general briefly explained the mysteries of the Catholic faith to the native chieftains. The caciques listened respectfully until Cortés urged them to destroy their pagan idols lest they burn eternally in hell.

The chieftains declined, saying their gods had long served them well, and warned that if the Spaniards defiled their temples the gods would surely kill them all at sea. Unimpressed by native curses,

Cortés's soldiers climbed to the temple's summit and smashed the idols. The conquistadors then enlisted some Indian artisans to help them build a Christian altar to accommodate an image of the Virgin Mary and also set up a large cross. The natives gazed intently as Father Juan Díaz, one of Cortés's company, conducted the island's first mass. Perhaps inspired by the majesty of the Spanish ceremony, the caciques asked Cortés to leave a priest behind so they could learn more of the new religion. The captain-general politely refused their request, fearing the natives might kill any priest he left with them. It was all quite simple, he told them. If they kept the cross clean, decorated it with flowers, and treated it with reverence, they would enjoy abundant crops and success in all that they did. Apparently, the natives took Cortés's instructions to heart. For years afterward, the islanders greeted Spanish ships by shouting "Cortés! Cortés!" and "María! María!"

On March 4, 1519, Cortés sailed again from Cozumel for Yucatán. Like a beast of prey, yet another gulf storm mauled the fleet during the night of the Spaniards' passage and then abated toward midnight. Sunrise revealed Yucatán's gleaming white beaches and striking signs of a civilization far more advanced than anything on Hispaniola or Cuba. As the Spanish ships glided along the coast, the soldiers saw neatly cultivated cornfields, and an occasional flat-topped temple would be visible above the trees. On one small cape, four tall statues of women kept silent watch for their unseen makers, causing the Spaniards to name the place the Cape of Women. Veterans of the Córdoba and Grijalva expeditions recognized Champoton, where the natives had killed so many of their number. Emboldened by the size of their army and anxious to avenge their dead comrades, many urged Cortés to land and punish the Indians. Outwardly, Cortés agreed with his men, but his chief pilot, Antón de Alaminos, knew the waters and advised the captain-general not to drop anchor where the fleet had so little protection against storms.

Tabasco

Secretly, Cortés probably welcomed Alaminos's advice. He had not risked his fortune simply to raid the coastal natives. Instead, he searched for a place where the conquistadors might trade and plant a settlement. Hoping to buy gold as Grijalva had, Cortés ordered the fleet to Tabasco. Since the Grijalva expedition, the Tabascans had reconsidered their policy toward the white men. Scolded by their neighbors for not attacking the intruders, the Tabascans now saw the Spanish ships and prepared to retrieve their lost honor in battle. As Cortés's fleet approached Tabasco, the Spaniards saw unmistakable signs of the Indians' hostility. Thousands of warriors, their faces blackened with warpaint, lined the shore. Log barricades blocked the approaches to the town, called Potonchan, and Indians rowed canoes near the fleet, warning the Europeans to leave or die. Díaz later wrote that he and the other veterans of Grijalva's expedition had expected a friendlier reception.

> The river, its banks, and the mangrove swamps were crowded with warriors, which greatly surprised us who had been here with Grijalva. In addition more than twelve thousand had gathered in town, all prepared to attack us.[19]

The Tabascans weren't dealing with Grijalva this time. Knowing he could not afford to appear weak if he intended to conquer this land, Cortés shouted back his determination to land and provision his fleet, peacefully if possible, by force if necessary. When the Indians became more defiant than ever, the Spaniards withdrew and during the night laid plans for battle. After questioning Grijalva's veterans about the town's layout, Cortés decided to attack with part of his forces advancing by land and the rest assaulting the defended shoreline.

"A Barrage of Indian Arrows"

The next morning when the Indians saw Cortés's men moving into position for their attack, they maneuvered their canoes to intercept. The native chieftains must have been confused when, with hostilities imminent, one of the Spaniards stepped to a ship's railing, unrolled a large scroll, and began reading to them in a loud voice. As he read, Aguilar translated each line into Mayan for the natives. As specified by Spanish law, the expedition's notary read the Requirement of 1513 to the Indians. This remarkable practice was designed to avoid bloodshed and protect the rights of natives. The lengthy document summarized history from the beginning of the world to the present, emphasizing the authority of the pope and of the Spanish king. At the end of the proclamation, the natives were invited to submit peacefully and become subjects of Charles I or suffer the consequences. Now if lives were lost, Cortés warned them, the fault would be theirs.

Shouting and taunting more loudly than before, the natives answered the Spaniards' declaration with a volley of arrows. Shouting "Santiago!" (Saint James), the conquistadors splashed ashore through a barrage of Indian arrows and javelins. In his account of the conquest, Díaz wrote respectfully of the warriors' resistance.

The whole bank was thick with Indian warriors, carrying their native arms, blowing trumpets and conches and beating drums. . . . With great bravery they surrounded us in their canoes, pouring such a shower of arrows on us that they kept us in water at some places up to our waists. There was so much mud and swamp that we had difficulty in getting clear of it; and so many Indians attacked us, hurling their lances and shooting arrows, that it took us a long time to struggle ashore.[20]

Despite the natives' determined defense, the conquistadors, with their superior weapons and organization, hacked their way to a plaza at the town's center. As the Indians retreated from the town, Cortés shouted that he claimed the land in the name of Charles I, raised his sword, and slashed a mark on a large tree to signify his claim. Diego Velázquez's followers grumbled that the captain-general had not claimed the land in the name of the governor. In the months ahead they would see far clearer evidence of Cortés's independent ways.

If Cortés's claim was controversial, his ability to make it good remained uncertain. Their numbers increased by reinforcements from the surrounding country, the Indians attempted to retake the town. The battle raged for days, the Tabascans pressing the attack, the Spaniards' crossbows, muskets, and swords taking a fearful toll on the Indians. Apparently thinking his Spanish masters faced certain defeat, the captive interpreter Melchior escaped and joined the Tabascans, offering them advice on how to fight the Spaniards. With the outcome in doubt, Cortés played his trump card. At a moment when neither side seemed able to gain an advantage, he disembarked his precious horses and prepared a cavalry charge. As Cortés expected, on March 25, 1519, the Tabascans renewed their attack.

Dressed in bright feathered robes and headdresses, their faces painted black and white, an estimated forty thousand warriors stretched across the open plain beyond the town. The little knot of Spanish soldiers plunged into the native horde, hoping to hold their attention until the cavalry surprised the Tabascans from the rear. Spanish cannon tore holes in the Indians' ranks, but still the Tabascans pressed forward through the dust and gun smoke. As the Spaniards desperately fought not for victory but survival, the blow fell—the first cavalry charge in North America.

Spanish and Aztec warriors lock in battle. Though greatly outnumbered, the conquistadors' superior weapons and horses would enable them to prevail.

The sight of the huge animals accomplished what gunfire and swordplay could not. Never having seen horses, the Indians believed horse and rider were a single, two-headed creature. Wherever the horsemen appeared the Indians fled. On one occasion, the appearance of a single cavalryman put thousands of Indians to flight, an event Cortés thought so miraculous that he believed the rider was actually Saint James descended from heaven to aid their cause. When the Tabascans retreated, Cortés knew the Indians were beaten. The battle, known as the Battle of Cintla, was over. The captain-general sent Indian prisoners to the Tabascan caciques asking for a peace council. The next day, the Indian bearers brought gifts of maize cakes, fruit, and turkeys to the Spaniards and announced that their chiefs would come the next day to talk peace.

Preying on Indian Fears

Intending to intimidate the Indians, Cortés ordered a mare in heat tied at the site where he planned to meet the chiefs and had a loaded cannon positioned nearby. After several hours, the mare was led away, but her scent remained. When the chiefs arrived the next day and met Cortés, at a prearranged signal one of the Spanish soldiers fired the cannon, sending a projectile crashing through the trees. Cortés then explained to the trembling chieftains that the cannon were still angry with the Indians and wanted to destroy them all, but that he had ordered the weapons to spare the Tabascans. Then another soldier led a stallion to the spot where the mare had been tied. Smelling

Spaniards on horseback pursue natives frightened by the sight. At first the natives thought horse and rider were one beast.

the mare, the horse began to rear and neigh loudly, and since the animal was facing the Indians, they believed his rage was directed against them. Cortés ordered the stallion led away and then assured the Indians that he had told the horses not to be angry with them.

After the conference, the caciques gave the horses gifts of roses and turkeys and begged their forgiveness. Cortés had successfully preyed on the Indians' fear of the unknown, a tactic that would serve the conquistadors well many times during the conquest. Now the Tabascans quickly became as loyal to Cortés as they had been hostile. During the days the Spaniards remained at Tabasco, the Indians fed them well and brought them gifts of slaves and golden objects.

Marina

Although the Spaniards at first did not realize it, the Tabascans had given them a gift far more valuable than gold—a slave named Malinche. A woman of exceptional beauty and intelligence, Malinche had grown up near Coatzacoalcos on the southeast edge of the Aztec kingdom. Her mother, the widow of a local chieftain, had remarried and gave Malinche away as a slave to make her son the family's sole heir. Living for years as a slave among the Tabascans, Malinche now spoke both Nahuatl, the language of the Aztecs, and Mayan. In 1518, Grijalva had communicated with the Aztecs solely through sign language. Now the Spaniards had an

Doña Marina

For centuries, historians have emphasized Marina's contribution to the Spaniards' success during the conquest. In this passage extracted from the nineteenth-century Conquest of Mexico, *William H. Prescott left a dramatic impression of this Indian princess.*

"One of the female slaves given [Cortés] by the Tabascan chiefs was a native Mexican, and understood the [Aztec's] language. Her name—that given to her by the Spaniards—was Marina; and . . . she was to exercise a most important influence on their fortunes. . . . It was not very long . . . before Marina, who had a lively genius, made herself so far mistress of the Castilian [Spanish] as to supersede the necessity of any other linguist. She learned it the more readily, as it was to her the language of love.

Cortés, who appreciated the value of her services from the first, made her his interpreter, then his secretary, and, won by her charms, his mistress. . . .

She is said to have possessed uncommon personal attractions, and her open, expressive features indicated her generous temper. She always remained faithful to the countrymen of her adoption; and her knowledge of the language and customs of the Mexicans, and more often of their designs [intentions], enabled her to extricate the Spaniards, more than once, from the most embarrassing and perilous situations."

effective, if complicated, means of communicating with the Aztecs. First Cortés would speak in Spanish to Aguilar, who would then speak in Mayan to Malinche, who finally translated into Nahuatl. Even a rough soldier such as Bernal Díaz recognized Malinche's contribution to the expedition's success. In his chronicle of the conquest he put it bluntly: "Without Dona Marina [Malinche] we could not have understood the language of New Spain and Mexico."[21]

Malinche's importance went far beyond her work as an interpreter. She became a Roman Catholic and took the Christian name Marina. Known to her Spanish companions as Doña Marina, a title implying nobility, she quickly became completely loyal to her liberators and did all she could to ensure their safety and success. Constantly at Cortés's side, in time she became his mistress and bore one of his sons. More than once her knowledge of Mexico's people saved the Spaniards. Ever alert, she warned them of ambushes. As cunning and calculating as the captain-general himself, she recommended strategies to exploit the natives' weaknesses. In fact, Marina and Cortés were so inseparable that the Indians eventually considered them a single superhuman being. Thus together they were called Malinche, a title that inspired awe and reverence among the Mexicans for decades following the conquest.

Like Malinche, the other slave women the Tabascans gave the Spaniards became Catholics, something Cortés required since some of the soldiers wished to take them as wives. The natives probably expected the victorious conquistadors to abduct their women and pillage at will, but Cortés, preparing the land and people for colonization, strictly forbade looting and rape. If the two peoples were to live together, peaceful intermarriage would help smooth relations between them. Early in the conquest, Cortés realized the importance of rewarding his friends and devastating his enemies. The Tabascans responded generously to the conquistadors' unexpected kindness. For

Marina acts as interpreter for Cortés. Marina's role was so important that some historians believe Cortés would not have been able to conquer the Aztecs without her.

the twenty days Cortés and his men rested at Potonchan, the Indians supplied them bountifully with food and occasionally with gold.

A Lust for Gold

The golden objects captivated the Spaniards. When questioned, the Indians made it clear that they knew nothing of gold mining, only picking up that which lay on the ground, and they placed comparatively little value on the yellow metal. When Cortés asked the natives where gold came from, they pointed to the west and said "Colua, Mexico." Since the Tabascans had little gold to offer, Cortés decided to search for a site suitable for colonization nearer the gold's source. In his biography of Cortés, Gómara writes that the captain-general's lust for gold drew him westward:

> With respect to the gold mines and treasures of the country . . . [the Tabascans said they] gave little importance to living as rich men, but only to be contented and happy, for which reason they could not even tell him

what a gold mine was; nor did they seek any gold but what they could pick up, which was very little; but that farther toward the setting sun a great deal of it was to be found. . . . [This knowledge] convinced Cortés that land was not for the Spaniards . . . so he decided to advance into the western country where the gold was.[22]

Before leaving Potonchan, Cortés, aided by his interpreters, persuaded the Indians to become subjects of Charles I, to accept Roman Catholicism, and to abandon human sacrifice. Doubtless impressed with the white men's power, the Tabascans readily agreed, although it is doubtful they fully understood their new allegiances. Following Cortés's orders, the natives destroyed their idols, and with the aid of Indian artisans the Spaniards built altars and crosses. On Palm Sunday, the conquistadors celebrated mass in as grand a fashion as their supplies allowed. Newly converted natives streamed into Potonchan by the thousands to join in the ceremony. Cortés had palm branches distributed to the worshipers and the Spaniards embarked on their vessels, waving the palm fronds as they left the Tabascans.

5 "Deeds So Marvellous"

By Holy Thursday, the fleet reached a protected harbor at San Juan de Ulua, a site just north of present-day Veracruz. There the Spaniards set up camp among the dunes, carefully fortifying it against surprise attack. Local Indians soon entered the camp, anxious to see the white men from another world. They seemed friendly enough, supplying the Spaniards with food and trading gold for trinkets such as beads, mirrors, and scissors. One, named Teudilli, commanded great respect from the rest. In Nahuatl, the language of the Aztecs, he informed Cortés that he governed this region at the pleasure of the great king Montezuma. The captain-general went to great pains to impress Montezuma's vassal, ordering Pedro de Alvarado to lead mock cavalry charges along the beaches and blasting away with his cannon. Cortés noticed that despite the natives' obvious fear of the horses and big guns, they recorded all they saw in paintings on cotton cloth. During one of his meetings with Cortés, Teudilli showed special interest in a helmet worn by one of the Spanish soldiers. Saying that it resembled one that rested on the idol of their

Cortés and Marina disembark at Veracruz, where Cortés would discover the vast wealth of Montezuma's empire and also that the emperor had many enemies.

A Disease of the Heart

At San Juan de Ulua, Cortés asked the Aztec governor Teudilli for gold, explaining that the Spanish obsession with gold was a disease. In Cortés, *Gómara says that Montezuma, learning of the Spaniards' lust for gold, tried to bribe the captain-general not to enter Tenochtitlán.*

"Cortés said: 'Send me some [gold] because I and my companions suffer from a disease of the heart which can be cured only with gold. . . .'

The governor [returned] with rich and beautiful presents: many . . . garments of white and colored cotton, embroidered in their fashion; many plumes and gorgeous feathers, richly and handsomely worked; a quantity of jewels and pieces of gold and silver; two thin disks, one of silver . . . representing the moon, the other of gold . . . representing the sun, with many decorations and animals carved upon it in relief, a very beautiful thing. . . .

[Teudilli said] that Cortés should determine what he needed for himself and the cure of his sickness, as well as for his men and ships . . . and that Moctezuma [Montezuma] would command that everything be faithfully provided; moreover, that if there was anything in the country that Cortés might wish to send to [Charles I], Moctezuma would . . . willingly give it to him. But, as for their meeting and talking together, he considered it impossible."

chief god, Huitzilopochtli, he asked if he could take it to his lord Montezuma. Cortés consented and asked that in return he fill it with gold dust so he could compare the gold of Mexico to that of his homeland. Teudilli agreed and promised he and his retainers would return in a few days with the gold sample and messages from his king.

After several days, Teudilli returned with thousands of native bearers bringing huge amounts of food, feather work, and gold. Previously, the Spaniards had traded for small amounts of gold frequently mixed with copper, often in the form of small jewelry or statuettes. Teudilli now brought outright gifts of gold and silver of excellent quality and in fabulous amounts. As Cortés had requested, he returned the helmet filled with fine gold dust. Most impressive were two disks as large as cartwheels, one carved in the image of the moon, the other fashioned into the likeness of the sun—the first of silver, the second of gold. With the gifts, Teudilli brought a message from Montezuma: He wished the Spaniards to stay on the coast and not to attempt to reach the Aztec capital, Tenochtitlán.

If the lord of the Aztecs believed the white intruders would be content with these gifts and leave his realms, he was sadly mistaken. Knowing now that Montezuma controlled wealth beyond his wildest dreams, Cortés became more determined than ever to enter the capital. He told Teudilli that Charles I, the lord of the lands across the sea, would be displeased if he did not meet Montezuma, about whom they had heard so much. It was also Charles's wish, he told Teudilli, that his people become Christians. After explaining the Catholic faith to Teudilli, Cortés gave him an image of the Virgin Mary and urged him to make an altar for it in Tenochtitlán. Teudilli's mood darkened at the suggestion, but he accepted the picture. When the Spaniards awoke in the morning, all the Aztecs were gone.

Cortés Ignores Risks

Thinking the Aztecs' sudden disappearance might be a prelude to attack, the ever alert Cortés ordered his men to strengthen their defenses. Many of the men grew nervous. Now in possession of more treasure than they had ever hoped, several argued that it was time to return to Cuba. Some were eager to return to their families and estates. Some were Velázquez's supporters and feared Cortés would take too much authority and profit for himself, denying the governor his share of the glory and gold. All of the Spaniards knew the risks life in the new land entailed. Thirty-five of their number had died in their battles with the Tabascans, and the Aztecs promised to be more numerous and powerful than the coastal Indians.

Cortés seemed indifferent to the risks. He hadn't invested all his resources just to raid Yucatán. His years in the Caribbean had taught him that lasting wealth was to be gained by becoming the governor of a profitable, well-administered colony. Cortés also felt obliged to save the natives from the darkness of paganism. After all, it was a conquistador's mission to convert people to the one true faith. However worthy these goals might be, Cortés's authority to establish a colony and conquer the Aztec domain remained questionable. Whatever Velázquez's real intentions were, his written instructions only authorized Cortés to trade with the natives. Even if the governor had hinted that he wanted Cortés to go beyond his written instructions and found a colony, the captain-general was not anxious to share either power or wealth with Velázquez. Drawing on his legal knowledge, Cortés solved the problem.

Cortés knew that even before the expedition had sailed, Velázquez had tried to establish his claims to the new lands. The governor had applied both to the colonial authorities in Hispaniola and directly to Charles I for permission to colonize Yucatán. Because of this, Cortés remained answerable to the governor, who in turn answered ultimately to the king himself. To gain more freedom to act, Cortés and his supporters voted to found a town. Since they had arrived at the site on Good Friday of the Cross, the conquistadors named the town Villa Rica de Vera Cruz (Rich Village of the True Cross) and appointed a town council to govern it. Cortés then resigned his commission from Velázquez as captain-general, freeing himself from the governor's authority. Finally, Villa Rica's council members elected Cortés captain-general, the chief military commander, of the new town.

Because of this complicated legal strategy, Cortés was now under the direct authority of the king and possessed the power to found colonies. To sweeten the deal, Villa Rica's council voted to give Cortés a share of all goods equal to that received by the king. When Velázquez's outvoted supporters complained that Cortés was no better than a mutineer, the new captain-general of Villa Rica threw them into chains. The captain-general appeased his less vocal opponents with generous amounts of gold. For the moment, the issue of who was in charge and whether the expedition would proceed inland was settled.

Cempoala

All that remained was to find a satisfactory site for the new town, since the camp among the dunes lacked an adequate harbor. As the conquistadors prepared to advance westward along the coast in search of a better location, Indian emissaries from the town of Cempoala arrived in camp. The men explained that they had not approached them earlier because they disliked and feared the Aztecs. The Cempoalans, a Totonac people, invited the Spaniards to visit them and refresh themselves in their town, an invitation Cortés happily accepted since the army's food stocks were running low.

In Cempoala, Cortés learned that the Aztecs had many enemies in their domain. The Cempoalan chief, nicknamed the Fat Cacique by the Spaniards, complained to the captain-general that the Aztecs ruled

their many provinces by terror, forcing their subjects into slave labor, exacting heavy taxes in food, gold, beautiful women for Montezuma's harem, and victims for human sacrifice. He told Cortés of Tenochtitlán, its vast size and wealth, huge armies, its impregnable defenses due to its location on a lake. Unintimidated by descriptions of Aztec power, Cortés delighted in the news that Montezuma ruled a kingdom ripe for revolt. According to Gómara:

> Cortés rejoiced to hear all this, which fitted in with his intentions, and he told the lord that he was sorry about the miserable treatment suffered by the land and people, but that the lord might be sure Cortés would put a stop to it and even avenge it, for he had come . . . only to right wrongs . . . favor the weak, and destroy tyrannies.[23]

If the people of Mexico were anxious to throw off their Aztec overlords, Cortés was only too happy to assist them. By embracing the Spaniards as liberators and fighting among themselves, the Indians would help bring about their own conquest.

Anxious to cement his alliance with the Spaniards, the Fat Cacique gave Cortés and his captains women to take as wives. In turn, Cortés insisted that the Cempoalans become Christians, a demand that the Fat Cacique rejected. Knowing that, like all the Indians they had encountered in the region, the Cempoalans routinely sacrificed humans to their idols, the chieftain's casual dismissal of the true faith enraged the conquistadors. Impulsively, several soldiers seized the chieftain and held him at swordpoint while their comrades bounded to the top of a temple and cast the native idols from the summit. At first shocked at

Conquistadors topple native idols. The Cempoalans became convinced of Cortés's power when such actions did not provoke an angry response from their gods.

the sacrilege, the native chief soon stood amazed that his gods did nothing to punish the white men. From that moment, the Cempoalans accepted the Spaniards' religion and remained steadfast in their devotion to these strangers who were greater than their gods.

Cortés and the Tribute Collectors

Accompanied by some Cempoalans, the Spaniards marched to Quiahuixtlán near the site where they intended to build Villa Rica. Once the Cempoalans explained who the Spaniards were, the townspeople received them in a friendly fashion, burning incense in clay braziers. Unknown to the Spaniards, the Indians performed this ritual for beings they considered gods. Like the Cempoalans, the caciques of Quiahuixtlán complained to Cortés of Montezuma's oppression. While the conquistadors were there, some Aztec tribute collectors swaggered into the town, ignoring the Spaniards and intimidating the townspeople. The Aztecs announced that the people of Quiahuixtlán had offended

The Spanish Policy of Forced Conversion

At Cempoala and throughout Mexico, the Spaniards converted Indians to Catholicism by force, a practice widely condemned throughout history. Richard Lee Marks, in this excerpt from Cortés: The Great Adventurer and the Fate of Aztec Mexico, *says the Spaniards found conversion through persuasion impractical.*

"The concept of conversion solely through education . . . by setting an example of Christian goodness had its history in the Spanish Church from the time of the Moors. . . . But the religious reeducation of the Moors by such means was rejected [because] there were not nearly enough Christian priests who could speak Arabic. . . . So . . . the Moors were subjugated by force . . . and Catholic ritual . . . was trusted to . . . maintain the forms of Christian worship while over the years Christian teaching would sink into the converts.

The situation in the New World was similar. There were hardly any priests fluent in the Indian tongues, and . . . the horrific nature of the Indian religion on the mainland made the threat of backsliding more to be dreaded; and there were many millions of Indians in countless tribes spread all over this vastness. Conversion through education and persuasion and by the setting of Christian example seemed too uncertain and slow. So most priests . . . accepted the soldiers' decision to command conversion and institute ritual."

the gods by harboring the bearded men and demanded twenty sacrificial victims in payment for their sins. Clearly the Aztecs were notifying all their subjects that no one was to offer the white strangers sanctuary.

Where others saw crises Cortés saw opportunities. The captain-general discreetly persuaded the cowering chiefs of Quiahuixtlán to arrest the emissaries and not to obey Montezuma or to pay taxes to him in the future. When one of the Aztecs resisted, he was flogged by his Cempoalan captors, something no one had dared to do to those who came in the name of the lord Montezuma. During the night, at Cortés's

command some soldiers helped two of the Aztecs slip away from their captors and brought them before the captain-general. Cortés assured them that he was sorry to see the emissaries of the great and good Montezuma abused by these rebellious people, so he arranged their escape. Providing the bewildered Aztecs with food for their journey, he urged them to return to their master with messages of his friendship and promised that he would guarantee the safety of the remaining Aztec prisoners. The escaping Aztecs, who expected to be sacrificed on their captors' altars, thanked the captain-general and fled into the night. When the caciques of Quiahuixtlán learned the Aztec prisoners had escaped and would surely bring news of their rebellion to Montezuma, terror overcame them. Still artfully playing his role, Cortés promised he would protect them from the Aztecs' reprisals. In one brilliant stroke, Cortés had befriended Montezuma and forced Quiahuixtlán into rebellion against the Aztecs. Now with Cempoala and Quiahuixtlán under his control, Cortés went from city to city among the Totonacs, recruiting allies against Montezuma. Each Spanish success since the Battle of Cintla had encouraged the Indians to believe the conquistadors were more than men. That the Spaniards were bold enough to humiliate the Aztecs and promise to free their tributary cities only enhanced the Spaniards' reputation. Díaz recounts:

> When they witnessed deeds so marvellous and of such importance to themselves they said that no human beings would dare do such things, and that it was the work of Teules, for so they call the idols which they worship, and for this reason from that time forth, they called us Teules, which is as much to say that we were either gods or demons.[24]

With the aid of Cempoalan laborers, the Spaniards began building Villa Rica not far from present-day Veracruz. More than a town, Villa Rica rose as a rough but defensible coastal fortress to be garrisoned by soldiers weakened by poor health or wounds. In short order the Europeans and Indians had erected a church, a jail, a town hall, and wharves for the harbor. As construction proceeded, a large group of Aztecs led by two of Montezuma's nephews entered Villa Rica. On behalf of their king, the young men thanked Cortés for helping his emissaries escape from Quiahuixtlán and gave him feather work, cotton garments, and gold. The captain-general obliged them by releasing the remaining prisoners to their custody. All this took place in plain view of the Cempoalans, who were amazed at the respect the Spaniards commanded. It appeared that Montezuma had sent tribute to Cortés, something unheard-of in all the Aztec realms. Were there no limits to the white men's powers?

Allegiance to Cortés Grows

More proof of their miraculous powers came soon enough. The Cempoalans complained that an Aztec garrison at Tizapantzinco had begun raiding their lands to punish them for rebelling against Montezuma. Without delay, Cortés assembled his men and with his Cempoalan allies marched on the Aztec fortress. The attack shocked the Aztecs, who had expected only to face the Cempoalans in battle. At the sight of the white men and their horses, Montezuma's legendary warriors fled. Soon the Spaniards overran Tizapantzinco, capturing many of the defenders. Fully expecting to be sacrificed by the Cempoalans and the people of the town they had occupied, the Aztecs found themselves disarmed and stripped of their pennants and battle standards but otherwise unharmed. At a critical moment, Cortés introduced an important new tactic to the region—he spared the defeated captives' lives but humbled them publicly. As news of the invincible Spaniards' compassion and the Aztecs' humiliation spread throughout the region, city after city pledged allegiance to Cortés and the great king of the east. Montezuma's domain hung like a piece of ripe fruit ready to fall into the Spaniards' open hands.

Cortés Destroys the Spaniards' Ships

Little did the Indians know that the Spaniards' own disunity threatened not only their success but their survival. Anxious to secure their claims to the new land, on July 26, 1519, the conquistadors sent a treasure ship directly to Spain with gifts and messages for Charles I. Along with the booty—which included the huge silver and gold disks, feather work, sculptures, and emeralds—Cortés sent several young Cempoalans. In its message to the king, the council of Villa Rica requested that Charles declare Cortés governor of New Spain (as they called the land).

Clearly Cortés intended to bypass Velázquez in all things concerning the expedition. Several of the governor's followers secretly plotted to hijack the vessel, kill its pilot, and deliver its golden cargo to Velázquez. Before they could board the ship and leave, the ever alert Cortés discovered their plot, forced confessions from the conspirators, and promptly tried and convicted them for mutiny. Two of the condemned men were hanged from Villa Rica's newly constructed gallows. Some conspirators suffered up to two hundred lashes, and one was sentenced to have his feet cut off. As brutal as the punishments seemed, Cortés spared most of

The Spaniards Promise Protection Against the Aztecs

Cortés encouraged rebellion against Montezuma and made alliances with the natives. In The Discovery and Conquest of Mexico, *Díaz says Cortés offered to protect the people of Quiahuixtlán when Montezuma learned they had refused to pay him tribute.*

"Cortés replied [to the caciques] with the most cheerful countenance that he and his brothers who were here with him would defend them and would kill anyone who tried to molest them. Then the Caciques and other townsmen vowed one and all that they would stand by us in everything we ordered them to do and would join their forces with ours against Montezuma and his allies. Then . . . they pledged obedience to His Majesty [Charles I] and messengers were sent to relate all that had happened to other towns in that province. And as they no longer paid any tribute and no more [Aztec] tax-gatherers appeared there was no end to the rejoicing at being rid of that tyranny."

Fearing a mutiny, Cortés has his ships destroyed and dismantled, trapping his soldiers.

the conspirators. With scarcely five hundred men under his command, a town to garrison, and an empire of unknown strength to conquer, the Spaniards could hardly afford to dispose of their own people. By making examples of the conspiracy's leaders, Cortés had reinforced his power to command, but a number of the conquistadors still grumbled that they wished to return to Cuba. According to Díaz, Cortés and his lieutenants devised a trick to avoid future incidents.

Conspiring with the captain-general, some of the pilots sabotaged the ships, gouging holes in their hulls. Then the pilots solemnly announced to the conquistadors that their vessels had rotted and become unseaworthy. With this grim declaration freshly in mind, Cortés ordered the worst ships dismantled, the salvageable ones beached, and the rigging and tackle stored. One serviceable vessel remained. Several of the sailors and soldiers openly questioned Cortés's motives and insisted they be allowed to sail to Cuba. Others also wished to return to Cuba but sullenly said nothing, fearing their comrades would call them cowards. Cortés generously announced that all who wished to leave could sail to Cuba in the remaining vessels. When the unhappy Spaniards who had remained silent accepted his offer, the captain-general ordered the last ship dismantled. Now he knew who his least reliable soldiers were, and he had removed their means of escape. Castaways in a hostile land, even the fainthearted among them would have to fight if they wished to survive.

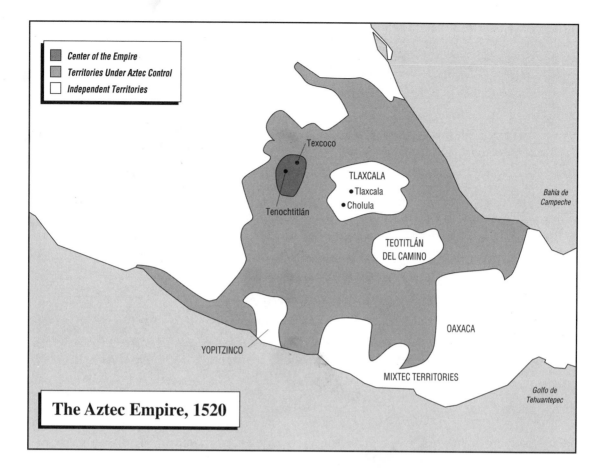

Center of the Empire
Territories Under Aztec Control
Independent Territories

Texcoco

TLAXCALA
• Tlaxcala
• Cholula

Tenochtitlán

TEOTITLÁN
DEL CAMINO

Bahía de
Campeche

YOPITZINCO

OAXACA

MIXTEC TERRITORIES

Golfo de
Tehuantepec

The Aztec Empire, 1520

With the debate about strategy temporarily over, Cortés made ready to march on Tenochtitlán. As the soldiers made their preparations, the captain-general received word that Francisco de Garay, the governor of Spanish Jamaica, had put scouts ashore near Villa Rica. Recognizing the threat Garay's claim posed to his own, Cortés captured Garay's scouts and through bribes persuaded them to join his little army. Knowing that for the moment Cortés held most of the advantages, the outnumbered Garay realized he had lost this round and sailed away. Time was running out. Cortés left his loyal friend Juan de Escalante in command of the Villa Rica

garrison and ordered the region's caciques to obey him and to finish building the town. Confident that Escalante would hold the town against any attacker, Indian or Spanish, the captain-general led his command into the mountains toward Mexico.

The Spaniards took along several of the Cempoalan caciques as guides. If the chieftains realized they also served as hostages to assure the safety of Villa Rica's garrison, they did not show it. Instead, they took obvious pleasure in traveling with the bearded ones from the land where the sun rises. In one city, the Indians asked the Cempoalans if these white men were gods. The Cempoalans happily confirmed the Spaniards' superhuman nature and warned that all who opposed them faced certain ruin.

"Piles of Human Skulls"

The more deeply they penetrated the Aztec realm, the more the conquistadors realized it was important that the Indians consider them supermen. Everywhere they looked the Spaniards saw evidence of the natives' ability to overwhelm the invaders. The conquistadors passed through cities with great stone temples and thousands of inhabitants. Chieftains dressed in plumed finery and accompanied by nobles in feathered robes brought them gifts of gold. With each step closer to Tenochtitlán, the wealth and beauty of the land increased. Each step also revealed scraps of sacrificial victims. The scraps became heaps, and the heaps became mounds. At one town, Díaz saw signs of human sacrifice on a scale that dwarfed even the bloody coastal regions.

> I remember that in the plaza . . . there were piles of human skulls so regularly arranged that one could count them, and I estimated them at more than a hundred thousand. I repeat again that there were more than one hundred thousand of them. And in another part of the plaza there were so many piles of dead men's thigh bones that one could not count them; there was also a large number of skulls strung between beams of wood.[25]

Silently, the soldiers read the meaning of these grim monuments to Mexican brutality: In the land of the Aztecs, defeat was not an option.

Even before leaving Villa Rica, Cortés understood that the expedition's success would depend heavily on recruiting Indian allies against the Aztecs. The Fat Cacique had assured Cortés that the Tlaxcalans would gladly join the Spaniards in their invasion of Mexico. Long surrounded by Montezuma's territory, the Tlaxcalans had maintained their independence through constant warfare with the Aztecs. Fierce, skilled in combat, and numerous, these mountain people seemed logical allies for the Spaniards. However, the Tlaxcalans' tradition of resistance had made them suspicious of foreigners. When the Spaniards marched toward the mountain republic, they found its border marked by a massive stone wall, nine feet tall and twenty feet thick. Stretching across a broad mountain valley, the wall silently warned all intruders to keep out. Unknown to the Spaniards, the Tlaxcalans knew Montezuma had sent messengers with gifts to Cortés. The Tlaxcalans considered any friends of the Aztecs their enemies. Their sudden attack fell on the Spaniards like a mountain storm.

The conquistadors had fought many kinds of Indians. They had slaughtered the natives of Hispaniola and Cuba like sheep. The Tabascans, despite their courage, had been broken by the Spanish cavalry. Nothing stopped the Tlaxcalans. Nothing frightened the Tlaxcalans. By the tens of thousands, trumpets blaring, warriors howling, they advanced with slingers, archers, and javelin throwers, ignoring cannon fire and cavalry. Four hundred Spaniards pressed forward through a blizzard of enemy arrows and spears, bravely fighting battles that never brought victory, only survival. None of Cortés's persuasive powers worked here. His peace offers rejected, his numbers daily decreasing from wounds, sickness, and exhaustion, Cortés buried his dead secretly at night to convince the enemy the Spaniards could not be harmed.

Outwardly, Cortés remained confident. When Aztec ambassadors arrived to observe the Spaniards' progress, Cortés calmly invited them to stay and see the conquistadors defeat Montezuma's enemies. Time, however, was clearly on the Tlaxcalans' side. In desperation, Cortés changed tactics. He dispatched detachments of soldiers to destroy undefended Tlaxcalan villages. Then at a conference with the enemy caciques, Marina and Aguilar warned them that the Spaniards would ravage the entire countryside if the Tlaxcalans did not submit. The warning came at a critical moment. The Tlaxcalans had tried everything against the Spaniards. When their magicians advised night attacks, the warriors found the Spaniards armed and ready to repel them. They sent spies to the Spanish camp disguised as peace emissaries, but Cortés, warned by Marina of their true intentions, returned them with their hands cut off. It seemed to the Indians that Cortés had the power to read their minds and anticipate their plans. Amazed that a handful of the bearded men had with-

Accompanied by his Tlaxcalan allies, Cortés and his cavalry march across the causeway leading into Tenochtitlán.

Following a predetermined signal from Cortés, conquistadors and Tlaxcalan warriors massacre the Cholulans.

stood their army for days, and fearful that their land would be devastated, the Tlaxcalans surrendered.

The Tlaxcalans embraced the white men as allies with the same determination they had fought them. Although the conquistadors remained alert to any sign of treachery, they found themselves well fed and offered every courtesy. Now convinced the Spaniards came to free the land from Montezuma's domination, the Tlaxcalans sent thousands of warriors to accompany Cortés to Tenochtitlán.

The Cholulan Massacre

The road to the Aztec capital led first to Cholula, a city sacred as the home of the native god Quetzalcoatl. Tlaxcala's caciques warned Cortés that the Cholulans were Montezuma's puppets and renowned for their treachery. After crossing high desert and coal-black lava beds, the Spaniards at last saw Cholula's gleaming white towers rising out of a green valley amidst the arid plains. At first the

Cholulans welcomed the conquistadors into their city, but after a few days Marina warned Cortés that Montezuma's ambassadors in the city had ordered the natives to ambush them as the Spaniards left the city for Tenochtitlán. After interrogations of Cholulan nobles confirmed her report, Cortés prepared a counterstroke.

The next day, with great fanfare, the Spaniards assembled in the city's plaza and prepared to leave. Thousands of Cholulans pressed into the town square. At a signal from Cortés, the conquistadors unsheathed their swords and attacked. Panicked Cholulans streamed from the plaza only to be mowed down by gunfire and Tlaxcalan warriors. After five hours, the slaughter ended, leaving as many as six thousand Cholulans dead.

In the presence of Montezuma's representatives, Cortés scolded the surviving Cholulan caciques for their treachery. Although the entire population deserved to be put to the sword, he said, he would spare the city further suffering out of respect for Montezuma. To the astonishment of both victors and vanquished, Cortés announced that all looting would cease and that the people of Cholula and Tlaxcala would hereafter be brothers. Under Spanish supervision, the Cholulans cleaned the gore of human sacrifice from their temples and set up crosses and images of the Blessed Virgin. With a last warning from Cortés that he would not treat the Cholulans' next rebellion so lightly, the Spaniards set out again for Tenochtitlán.

As word of the Spanish triumphs spread from the coast to the mountains, one question dominated the Indians' thoughts: Who were these men who fought like demons, knew their enemies' thoughts, and dared challenge not only the lord of the Aztecs but the gods he served?

Chapter

6 "I Am He"

In Tenochtitlán, the lord of the Aztecs trembled with fear. They were coming. Day after day relay runners arrived with reports of the white strangers' progress. At a distance of over two hundred miles from the coast, Montezuma knew of the Tabascans' defeat, the Totonacs' rebellion, Tlaxcala's alliance with the Spaniards, and the massacre in Cholula. Perhaps the ancient prophecies were to be fulfilled in his lifetime.

According to Aztec legend, in the distant past the great god Quetzalcoatl had brought peace, prosperity, and knowledge to the people of Middle America. From him they learned writing, weaving, pottery making, stone sharpening, and improved agricultural techniques. Legend held that during Quetzalcoatl's reign in Mexico, ears of corn grew as long as a man's body. Traditionally a god of peace, Quetzalcoatl banned human sacrifice, instead instructing his people to offer butterflies and reptiles on their altars. His was a message of love, teaching that all men are brothers. For twenty years, Quetzalcoatl ruled Cholula until he was driven out by hostile gods, under whose rule men turned once again to human sacrifice. Then he and his followers embarked on a boat, vowed to return one day to reclaim his domain, and sailed across the water to the land where the sun rises. According to the prophets,

he would appear as a white-skinned, bearded man traveling on white wings across the water and would return in the Aztec year One Reed—the year known to the Spaniards as A.D. 1519.

The feathered serpent that represents the Aztec god Quezalcoatl. The Aztecs believed that Cortés might be Quezalcoatl, returning in human form.

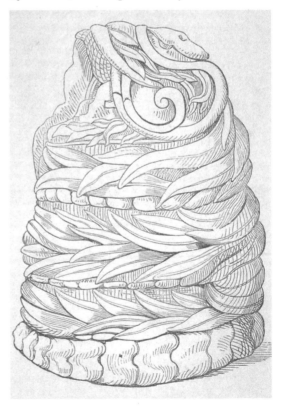

Montezuma Fears the White-Skinned Gods

Historians still debate why Montezuma, the most powerful of the Aztec rulers, did so little to stop Cortés's army from entering Tenochtitlán. According to this excerpt from the General History of the Things of New Spain *translated from Aztec texts by Fray Bernardino de Sahagún, the lord of the Aztecs feared the Spaniards were gods against whom he was powerless.*

"And when he had . . . heard what the messengers reported, he was terrified. . . . Especially did it cause him to faint away when he heard how the gun [cannon], at [the Spaniards'] command . . . resounded as if it thundered. . . . Fire went showering forth. . . . And when [the shot] struck a mountain, it was as if it were . . . dissolved. . . .

In iron they [the Spaniards] clothed themselves. . . . And those [horses] which bore them upon their backs, their deer, were as tall as roof terraces. . . .

And when Moctezuma had . . . heard that . . . the gods wished to look upon his face, it was as if his heart was afflicted. . . . He wished to flee. . . .

But this he could not do. . . . No longer had he strength. . . .

[Moctezuma] only awaited [the Spaniards]; he made himself resolute . . . he controlled his heart; he submitted himself entirely to whatsoever he was to see, at which he was to marvel."

As the year approached, Montezuma saw grim omens. Fire blazed across the sky. Violent waves on Lake Texcoco, which surrounded Tenochtitlán, flooded the city and destroyed houses. Popocatepetl, a long-dormant volcano, rumbled, smoked, and shook the earth. Lightning from a gray, drizzling sky destroyed the temple of Huitzilopochtli, the Aztec war god. A madwoman wandered the capital's streets at night wailing warnings of imminent disaster. Perhaps strangest of all, a bird with a small mirror on its forehead was brought to Montezuma. Gazing into the mirror, the Aztec ruler saw white men mounted on large deer.

Prophecies haunted the lord of the Aztecs all his life. Early in his reign, one of his courtiers warned him that the kingdom would fall during his lifetime. More than once, Montezuma confessed that he served only as caretaker of the domain until the gods decreed otherwise. Now the omens hinted that time might have come. In his own mind, he had been a good steward of the Aztec realms. Fearless in combat, Montezuma led his armies to victories that made the Aztec kingdom larger than ever before. The capital's storehouses bulged with treasure. His tribute collectors brought food, firewood, gems, slaves, concubines, and sacrificial victims to Tenochtitlán.

During his reign, countless thousands of sacrificial victims, torn from their homes in the 371 towns that paid the Aztecs tribute, had been slain on Tenochtitlán's altars. Montezuma's gods demanded no less. His own coronation required the ritual slaughter of over five thousand people. Montezuma had fed the gods well. He was more than a king to his people. Montezuma was a high priest, and like his subjects he believed that the world might be destroyed at the end of every fifty-two-year cycle unless the Aztecs offered the gods human blood. Seemingly, the more blood the gods consumed, the greater the guarantee of safety for mankind. The year One Reed ended one of those cycles. Now, obsessed with superstition, Montezuma heard reports of bearded white strangers who swept all opposition before them, united ancient enemies, preached liberation, and abolished human sacrifice—and they came in huge ships from the land where the sun rises.

Hoping Cortés was not Quetzalcoatl but fearing that he was, Montezuma desperately tried to determine the captain-general's identity. Having seen the ships, the giant deer (horses) the white strangers rode, the thunder and lightning from their muskets and cannon, the messengers sent word to Montezuma—surely Cortés must be the god of prophecy or, at least, his messenger.

Aztecs perform human sacrifice to feed their gods. The Aztecs believed such sacrifice was necessary to appease their gods' hunger for human blood.

Aztec Human Sacrifice

The Aztecs terrorized their subjects, taking thousands for human sacrifices. Ironically, this ritual sacrifice grew out of the Aztecs' own fear that without gifts of blood the world might risk destruction every fifty-two years. In this excerpt from The Aztec: Man and Tribe, *Victor W. von Hagen explains the reasons for the bloody Mexican religion.*

"The dominant note was the fifty-two-year cycle; the whole of the tribe's intellectual forces was put to work long before its advent to allay the wrath of the gods.

The priests had to calculate ritual by the most involved methods; they had to know the precise interconnection between each particular god and 'time' as given on the calendar. Sacrifice had to be correctly calculated so that it would benefit the particular god to whom they were appealing. All the developed intellect of the Aztec was turned toward this one thing: how to propitiate [gain the favor of] the right god at the right time. So sacrifice was not mere butchery, it was a parade of elaborately conceived ritual with only one object in view: to preserve human existence."

The Aztecs believed that killing their enemies in ritual sacrifice preserved their people's existence.

As a devoted follower of the Aztec gods, Montezuma knew he should rejoice at Quetzalcoatl's return and the fulfillment of prophecy, but he also knew it meant the end of his reign. His attempts to keep the strangers out of Tenochtitlán revealed his confusion and despair. He offered bribes to Cortés, complained that he was too ill to meet the Spaniards, warned that the trip was too dangerous for the Europeans, claimed that food was too scarce in the capital to sustain the visitors, and attempted treachery and ambush at Cholula. Never did he gamble that the Spaniards were merely men and he could send his massive army to annihilate them. Paralyzed by fear and indecision, he now found the intruders at his gates.

The Spaniards Enter Tenochtitlán

Cortés suffered no lack of resolve. Emboldened by success, he braved forbidding mountain terrain, ignored Aztec warnings, suppressed his own men's fears, and pressed on. Thanks to Marina's and Aguilar's counsel, he also now understood that the natives widely regarded him and his men as gods, an impression that gained him friends and demoralized his enemies. According to Díaz, even in the heart of the Aztec realm, the Indians viewed the Spaniards as liberators.

[The caciques] secretly, so that the Mexican Ambassadors should not hear them, made great complaints about Montezuma, and his taxgatherers, who robbed them of all they possessed, and carried off their wives and daughters, and made the men work as though they were slaves . . . and took their lands for the service of their Idols. . . .

Cortés comforted them with kindly words . . . but added that . . . they must bear it awhile and he would presently free them.[26]

As the army emerged from the mountain passes, the Spaniards beheld the Valley of Mexico. In the distance lay Tenochtitlán, a city of white stone on a sapphire blue lake, the focal point of power and wealth in Middle America.

As the sun rose on November 8, 1519, the little Spanish army and as many as six thousand Indian allies crossed the two-mile causeway spanning Lake Texcoco and through the fortress gates into Tenochtitlán. Hundreds of Indians anxious to see the strangers paddled canoes onto the lake from the capital's canals. The sight must have overwhelmed the rough Spanish soldiers. Far larger than any city in Spain, the Aztec capital, resting on an island, could be approached only across narrow stone causeways or by canoe and was both easy to defend and difficult to escape. Massive flat-topped temples dominated the skyline. Some buildings shone white in the morning sun while others sported murals in bright reds, blues, and greens.

Hundreds of Aztecs in brilliant plumed finery approached the Spaniards in solemn procession. Several, eyes downcast to show reverence for their master, carried a golden litter bearing Montezuma. Once they reached Cortés, the litter bearers stopped and their royal passenger stepped down. Mats were spread in his path to keep his feet from touching the pavement. Resplendent in

Cortés and his mounted conquistadors meet Montezuma and his elaborate entourage at Tenochtitlán.

clothes decorated with gems and trimmed with gold and silver, Montezuma hung a golden necklace around Cortés's neck, an act that astonished his retainers. Never had they seen the lord of the Aztecs touch another human in public. Unruffled by the honor, Cortés greeted Montezuma and gave him a necklace of pearls and glass beads. In his translation of Aztec texts, Bernardino de Sahagun describes the scene:

> Moctezuma . . . gave gifts to the commandant [Cortés] . . . he bejeweled him with necklaces, he hung garlands about him. . . . Thereupon he had the golden necklaces laid before him . . . with which the meeting was concluded. . . .

Then [Cortés] said to Moctezuma: "Is this not thou? Art thou not he? Art thou Moctezuma?"

Moctezuma replied: "Indeed yes; I am he."[27]

At Montezuma's command, the Spaniards and their Indian auxiliaries were escorted to a palace large enough to house them all. Cortés thanked God for permitting his safe entry into the city but took precautions for the army's safety. His

Indian allies and several of the caciques in Aztec territory had repeatedly told him that Montezuma would kill all the Spaniards once he had them in his power. With these warnings in mind, the captain-general ordered the palace converted into a fortress. Cannon guarded all approaches to the building, soldiers stood constant watch, and no one was to wander out of the Spaniards' quarters without permission. That night, the roar of cannon echoed across the lake as the conquistadors celebrated their entry into the Aztec capital.

The Great Temple

With the intruders effectively trapped in the city, Montezuma did nothing to harm them. In fact, he bluntly told Cortés that he believed the white men had come from the ruler of the land where the sun rises, implying that he meant Quetzalcoatl, and acknowledged that the Aztec realm was now his to command. The Aztec ruler seemed anxious to show Cortés his domain and led him on a tour of the capital. Wide-eyed, the Spaniards strolled through the marketplace, where tens of thousands of natives conducted the commerce of the empire. The conquistadors marveled at the straight, paved streets, at the apparent absence of crime, and at the city's cleanliness. At Montezuma's invitation, Cortés and several of his soldiers ascended the Great Temple. A pyramid over one hundred feet tall, the temple towered above Tenochtitlán's skyline and provided a clear view of the entire city. More importantly, on this massive structure the whole city could see Mexico's gods receive gifts from their followers.

The Great Temple rises above Tenochtitlán. The sight of the temple's sanctuary, its walls clotted with blood, appalled the conquistadors.

Montezuma led his guests into a sanctuary on the temple's summit. The stench of death filled the room. Priests clad in filthy black robes, their dark hair hanging in tangled masses hurriedly went about their business, ignoring Montezuma's guests. The nature of that business soon became obvious. In the dimly lit sanctuary, the conquistadors saw three human hearts sizzling in a brazier, each recently torn from its owner's chest. Looking around the room, the Spaniards realized that fresh blood dampened the floor and the walls were thickly encrusted with clotted blood. A grinning stone idol of the Aztec war god, Huitzilopochtli, stood silently unaware of the gory feast.

The soldiers had seen suffering and death on the battlefield, but sickened by this grisly scene, they fled to the open air. As calmly as possible, Cortés approached Montezuma and suggested that the gods he worshiped were actually devils. He urged the Aztec ruler to accept Catholicism, cleanse the temple, and erect a cross and altar with an image of the Virgin Mary. Shocked at the insult to his gods, Montezuma protested that Cortés had committed sacrilege and told the Spaniards to leave.

For the moment, Cortés decided not to press the issue. Instead, with Montezuma's consent Cortés's carpenters built an altar at the Spanish quarters, so the soldiers could properly celebrate mass. As the construction proceeded, workmen noticed that a wall seemed to have been recently plastered. On Cortés's orders, the men broke through the plaster and entered a hidden room. The soldiers stood amazed at the room's contents. Mounds of gems, silver objects, and golden statuary filled the room. They had stumbled across Montezuma's treasure. Cortés ordered the room resealed and nothing said to the Aztecs about the discovery. He would use this knowledge when the right moment arose.

The Spaniards Take Montezuma Hostage

Each day the men who wished to return to Cuba grew more nervous about their situation. All the soldiers now realized they had never encountered a native ruler who wielded this sort of power. Deep inside Montezuma's capital, surrounded by a population of 250,000 Aztecs who cannibalized their captives, some soldiers became anxious to loot the treasury and escape to the coast.

Cortés acknowledged the danger but argued that fleeing Tenochtitlán would only expose them to attack on the long and difficult return trip to Villa Rica. Aside from that, the captain-general and his supporters had not come to Mexico merely to loot and return to Cuba. They intended to conquer the country, Christianize its people, and develop its resources. Early in the expedition Cortés had considered seizing Montezuma. Now a pretext for doing so presented itself. Tlaxcalan messengers arrived in Tenochtitlán and told Cortés that Aztec warriors had killed six Spaniards near Villa Rica. Fearful that the natives would conclude that the conquistadors were not invincible and begin to pick them off a few at a time, Cortés and his officers decided to arrest Montezuma immediately.

By now Montezuma was accustomed to armed Spaniards entering and leaving his

Crusaders in America

As greedy as Cortés and his men were, they also willingly risked their lives to advance God's kingdom on earth. In this passage from The Conquistadors: First-Person Accounts of Mexico, *translated by Patricia de Fuentes, a soldier named Andrés de Tapia notes Cortés's determination to set up a Catholic altar in Tenochtitlán.*

"The images were of idols, and in their mouths and over parts of their bodies were quantities of blood two or three fingers thick.

When the marques [Cortés] . . . sighed saying . . . 'Oh God! Why do You permit such great honor paid the Devil in this land? Look with favor, Lord, upon our service to You here.'

He called . . . some of the priests of those idols . . . and he said . . . 'Here where you have these idols I wish to have the images of the Lord and His Blessed Mother. Also bring water to wash these walls, and we will take all this away.'

They laughed as though it were not possible to do such a thing, and they said . . . 'This is the house of Uchilobos [Huitzilopochtli] whom we serve. . . . The people . . . on seeing you come up here . . . have all risen in arms and are ready to die for their gods. . . .'

Then [Cortés] said to the priests: 'It will give me great pleasure to fight for my God against your gods, who are a mere nothing. . . .'

I swear . . . that . . . the marques leaped supernaturally, and, . . . he reached as high as the idol's eyes and thus tore down the gold masks [from the idol] saying: 'Something we must venture for the Lord.'"

presence. After warning his men to be doubly alert to Aztec attack, Cortés, his interpreters, and about thirty of his men casually filtered into the Aztec king's palace. After some friendly conversation, Cortés suddenly accused Montezuma of treacherously ordering an attack on his men and insisted the king be imprisoned in the Spanish quarters. Shocked by the accusation, Montezuma protested his innocence and refused to cooperate. Cortés and the Aztec monarch argued for hours until an exasperated conquistador named Juan Velásquez shouted, "Let us either take him prisoner, or stab him, tell him once more that if he cries out or makes an uproar we will kill him!"[28]

When Montezuma turned to Marina and asked what Velásquez had said, the native beauty warned him that his life was in danger. Díaz credits Marina with bringing an end to the impasse:

Cortés shackles Montezuma to prevent the emperor from escaping after taking him prisoner.

As Dona Marina was very clever, she said: "Senor Montezuma, what I counsel you, is to go at once to their quarters without any disturbance at all, for I know that they will pay you much honour as a great Prince such as you are, otherwise you will remain here a dead man."[29]

Seeing himself surrounded by these white warriors who worked miracles, the lord of the Aztecs quietly went into captivity.

Day by day it became more obvious to both the Spaniards and the Aztecs that Cortés controlled Montezuma. The Aztec nobles who had killed the conquistadors at Villa Rica were seized, tried under Spanish law, and publicly burned at the stake in Tenochtitlán. Significantly, Cortés used wooden weapons from the capital's armory to kindle the fire. When rumors circulated that one of Montezuma's nobles intended to launch an attack to free the Aztec king, Montezuma removed him from his command and appointed a replacement acceptable to Cortés. Aztec carpenters helped the Spaniards build two brigantines (small sailing ships) on Lake Texcoco, providing the conquistadors a means of escape if the Aztecs blocked the causeways. The people of Tenochtitlán watched as their semidivine ruler, closely guarded by Spanish soldiers, cruised the lake in the strange European vessels.

Cortés Demands More Riches

Montezuma still met with his courtiers and attended to the business of the empire, but he had become a hostage in his own capital. Although Cortés never claimed godhood, more than once Montezuma openly recognized the captain-general as the divine one, or the servant of the divine one, who had come to rule Mexico. Now, at Cortés's command, Montezuma assembled his nobles and formally abdicated his throne to the white lord from the east. One by one, the sobbing nobles swore their allegiance to Cortés and his sovereign, Charles I.

Having tamed the lord of the Aztecs, Cortés increased his demands. He reminded Montezuma of King Charles's desire for tribute and suggested that the room of treasure his men had found would make an appropriate gift. Without hesitation, Montezuma gave the entire treasure to Cortés and apologized for its small size. The Aztec ruler then ordered more gold and silver gathered from distant mines and tributary cities to increase his gift to the ruler across the sea

The windfall intensified divisions among the soldiers. They had endured tropical heat, mosquitoes, bitter cold, barren deserts, and risked their lives in pitched battles, but had received little of the wealth Cortés had promised. Most of the booty they had seized had been sent to King Charles, leaving them only a few baubles to show for their efforts, yet Cortés always had gold to bribe those he wished to persuade. Against Cortés's advice, the soldiers demanded their share of Montezuma's treasure. Reluctantly, the captain-general agreed, dividing the treasure among his men according to their rank. Cortés took his fifth, while officers, harquebusiers (musketeers), and cross-bowmen received more than common soldiers. Many soldiers grumbled that Cortés had cheated them but for the moment accepted their allotments. In short order, priceless Aztec sculptures were melted down into ingots and chains that each soldier carried with him. Little did the conquistadors know that few would leave Mexico with their newfound wealth.

Spaniards Fight Spaniards

The Spaniards had already accomplished more than they had dreamed possible. Poised to consolidate their power and conquer the empire from within, they suddenly faced a new threat from without. A cheerful Montezuma told Cortés more ships carrying his white brothers had landed on the coast. While in Montezuma's presence, the captain-general praised God for their arrival, but he sensed trouble. Cortés's scouts soon returned and confirmed his fears. Governor Velázquez had sent one of his lieutenants, Pánfilo de Narváez, with a force at least three times larger than that of Cortés. Not only did Narváez have orders to arrest Cortés for mutiny, but he had already sent word to Montezuma that all the Spaniards would leave Mexico once Cortés was in chains.

Without hesitation, the captain-general left Pedro de Alvarado with a small detachment to garrison the capital, and then he marched with the remainder of his command and some Tlaxcalan warriors to deal with Narváez. Always the master of psychological warfare, Cortés sent messengers ahead of his column with bribes of gold to Narváez and his key officers, hinting that there was more to come if they joined him. Narváez foolishly took the gold for himself and boasted that he would easily dispose of the mutineers. For the moment, he and his men camped at Cempoala and passed the time by looting the Indians and taking their women. Enraged by the Spaniards' abuse, the Fat Cacique warned Narváez that Cortés was no mortal man. Malinche, he said, would destroy the invaders without warning, and justice would be done.

After an exhausting forced march, Cortés's men halted on a rainy night three miles from Narváez's camp. The captain-general's scouts reported that Narváez's forces held at least a four-to-one advantage and possessed many cannon. According to a soldier named Andrés de Tapia, Cortés told his men Narváez had offered him peace terms advantageous to him but not to them. He asked them if they preferred to fight or submit:

"I . . . can speak for no more than one man [said Cortés]. The matter rests with each one of you. Whether it is your inclination to fight or to seek peace, speak your mind and no one shall hinder you from doing as you wish. . . ."

Unanimously we gave a shout of Joy, saying: "Hurrah for our captain . . . !" Then we picked him up and carried him on our shoulders until he had to beg us to let him go.[30]

Cortés launched his attack that night in the rain, something unusual for sixteenth-century armies. Surprise was total. Awakened by the crack of musket fire, Narváez's troops blundered through the darkness, groping for their weapons. Even nature sided with Cortés. The defenders mistook fireflies flushed from the grass by the attackers for burning cords on matchlocks and thought they were surrounded by hundreds of harquebusiers. Some cavalrymen leaped to their horses only to crash to the ground because Cortés's men had cut their cinch straps. From the top of a temple, Narváez roared encouragement to his troops only to suffer a pike (spear) wound to the eye. Howling in agony, he fell captive, leaving his men leaderless.

It ended quickly. With their commander struck down and Cortés's veterans everywhere victorious on the battlefield, Narváez's men surrendered. The captain-general offered the captive army two choices—be put to the sword or join him and share the Aztec treasure. To a man, the prisoners swore loyalty to their captor. Now in command of over one thousand men, Cortés ordered Narváez's ships disabled and marched his troops westward.

On the way, Tlaxcalan runners brought word that the Aztecs had risen up and laid siege to Alvarado and his men. Cortés confidently announced that he would soon set everything right and quickened the army's pace. If Narváez's men were bewitched by the captain-general's promises of wealth and glory, Cortés's veterans knew the danger ahead. Writing of the newcomers, Díaz said, "If they had known the power of Mexico, it is certain that not one of them would have gone."[31]

7 A Notable Feat of Arms

On June 24, 1520, Cortés's reinforced Spanish army marched into Tenochtitlán. Unlike their triumphal entry into the capital the previous fall, no Aztec nobles greeted them. Instead, a handful of natives occupied the city streets. Here and there the conquistadors saw some of the smaller bridges were destroyed, an ominous sign. An eerie silence hung over the greatest city of the New World. In his *Conquest of Mexico*, William Prescott describes the Spaniards' return to Tenochtitlán:

> How different was the scene from that presented on his former entrance! No crowds now lined the roads, no boats swarmed on the lake, filled with admiring spectators. . . . A deathlike stillness brooded over the scene—a stillness that spoke louder to the heart than the acclamations of multitudes.[32]

The streets echoed with the clatter of horses' hooves on pavement and the rattle of metal weapons against armor. It was as if the whole city lay coiled like a giant serpent ready to strike out at the returning Spaniards. On Cortés's orders, the Spanish trumpeters sounded and were soon answered by the roar of cannon from within the city. At least Alvarado and his men were still alive.

Once the Spaniards had safely entered their fortified quarters, Montezuma greeted Cortés and apologized for the fighting. After exchanging a few pleasantries, the captain-general sought out Pedro de Alvarado. Apologetically, Alvarado explained that he had granted the Aztec priests permission to celebrate the feast of Huitzilopochtli on the condition that the Indians sacrifice no humans. When thousands of bronze-skinned revelers filled the streets, Alvarado panicked, thinking the frenzied natives would attack his tiny command. Always impetuous, Alvarado struck first. On his orders, Spanish horsemen charged into the streets, cutting down hundreds of worshipers with their Toledo blades. The Aztecs, outraged at the unprovoked attack, armed themselves and charged, driving the outnumbered Spaniards back into their fortified palace. Only when Montezuma appeared on a rooftop and appealed for peace did the attacks end.

Now the city's silence made sense to Cortés. The natives had permitted the army to reenter Tenochtitlán so they could capture all the Spaniards. The conquistadors were trapped. For the moment, Cortés said little of his lieutenant's stupidity. Not only did he need every soldier to fight the Aztecs, he needed every reliable man to control the fainthearted and disloyal among his own men. Before retiring, the captain-general inspected the palace and found it well secured, with guards in place and cannon manned. At least Alvarado had wisely dug a well within the fortress's walls to provide the army a secure source of water. Cortés considered his options.

Flushed with confidence from his earlier successes, the captain-general assumed that his enlarged army could quickly restore the city to Spanish control. At dawn the next morning, the Aztec warriors massed around the Spanish quarters, firing arrows and throwing stones from nearby buildings. Suddenly the fortress gates burst open. Cortés's cavalry, followed by foot soldiers and Tlaxcalan allies, surged into the street and slashed through the Indian legions. After recovering from the shock of the Spanish attack, the Aztecs swarmed Cortés's detachment, dragging some riders from their mounts, even clinging to the horses' legs to keep the cavalry from maneuvering. As the Spanish charge ground to a halt, Cortés's force wheeled and fought its way back into the fortress. Safe within their quarters' walls, the weary Spaniards could hear Aztec warriors taunting them, boasting that Huitzilopochtli would soon feast on the white men's flesh.

The Death of Montezuma

The next morning, thousands of warriors again showered the fortress with arrows. Shaken by the Aztecs' fierce determination, Cortés persuaded Montezuma to call on his people to leave the Spaniards in peace. Reluctantly, the lord of the Aztecs, dressed in

his finest robes, golden sandals, and clasps encrusted with emeralds, ascended a rooftop and faced his subjects. At the sight of their ruler, the Indian multitudes fell silent. Many fell to their knees and cast their eyes downward when faced with his sacred presence. In measured tones, Montezuma began to speak to his subjects. Sullen voices rumbled through the crowd. Soon they rose to a roar and drowned out Montezuma's speech.

"Coward!" shouted someone from the crowd. As a volley of arrows and stones arced through the air, Spanish soldiers tried to shield their royal captive but were too late. Montezuma fell, severely wounded, and was carried inside by his

Montezuma is attacked by his own people for being a coward and surrendering to the Spaniards. The attack ended the conquistadors' hope that they could use Montezuma as a hostage to escape.

The Fury of the Aztecs

Having returned to Tenochtitlán after defeating Narváez, the Spaniards found the Aztecs were now determined to destroy them. In Conquest of Mexico, *William H. Prescott describes the Aztec siege of the conquistadors' quarters.*

"The undaunted Aztecs hung on the rear of their retreating foes, annoying them every step by fresh flights of stones and arrows; and when the Spaniards re-entered their fortress, the Indian host encamped around it. . . . During the night, they broke the stillness of the hour by insulting cries and menaces, which reached the ears of the besieged. 'The gods have delivered you, at last, into our hands,' they said; 'Huitzilopochtli has long cried for his victims. The stone of sacrifice is ready. The knives are sharpened. . . . And the cages,' they added, taunting the Tlascalans [Tlaxcalans] with their leanness, 'are waiting for the false sons of Anahuac [Mexico] who are to be fattened for the festival.'"

captors. For three days he lingered in great pain, refusing treatment from the Spaniards. A Spanish priest urged Montezuma to accept the Catholic faith and be baptized, but the dying king remained true to his ancestors' religion to the end. On June 30, 1520, the lord of the Aztecs died in the company of the men who wished to steal his kingdom.

The Sorrowful Night

Cortés assembled his men and outlined a situation they knew only too well. Without Montezuma as a hostage, nothing but their own fighting skills would hold the Aztecs in check. Food was scarce, they could expect no reinforcements, and the enemy had destroyed the causeway bridges. Since the Aztecs seldom fought at night, the army would steal away in the darkness and use a portable wooden bridge to span the gaps in the causeways. The king's share of the treasure would be loaded on horses. As for the rest, the men could help themselves, but they should take only small amounts so they could travel quickly. Cortés's veterans heeded this warning, but Narváez's men, astounded at the mounds of treasure, soon staggered under heavy loads of gold. It was a decision many would soon regret.

Marching through a drizzling rain, the army reached the first gap in the causeway and bridged it without interference. Unfortunately, the passing army's weight so deeply embedded the bridge in the mud that it could not be moved. As the Spaniards struggled to free the bridge, Indian sentries heard the commotion and roused the city's defenders. Immediately, thousands of Aztec warriors charged down

The battle referred to as the Sorrowful Night was sorrowful only for the Spaniards and their Tlaxcalan allies—two-thirds of them died. For the Aztecs, the battle was a triumph.

the causeway, and countless more assaulted Cortés's men from canoes. Chaos reigned. Arrows and javelins fell on the Spaniards in the darkness. Both soldiers and Tlaxcalans rushed to the next gap in the causeway, plunged into the water, and tried to scramble up the muddy slope. Dying men, weighted down by armor and Aztec gold, soon formed a grisly, writhing bridge that their comrades crossed in a mad rush to safety.

Perhaps two-thirds of the Spaniards and Tlaxcalans died in the battle. To this day no one knows the exact number. None of the survivors escaped unwounded. The remnant of Cortés's army collapsed exhausted on the lakeshore. All their cannon, muskets, and many of their crossbows had been lost. Behind them, most of Montezuma's treasure lay buried in the muck at the bottom of the lake. Screams of their dying comrades mingling with the Aztec le-

gions' triumphant shouts echoed across the water. In the annals of the conquest, this night would forever be called the Noche Triste—the Sorrowful Night.

The Battle of Otumba

For the moment, the Aztecs were too busy killing the wounded and taking captives into the city for sacrifice to pursue the Spaniards. Realizing their only hope for safety lay in reaching Tlaxcala, Cortés pushed his command toward the mountains as rapidly as its condition allowed. For a week Aztec raiding parties nipped at the fleeing army's heels, occasionally closing in to attack stragglers. Now and then a bold warrior taunted the Spaniards, ominously urging them to hurry forward to their deaths. The army passed San Juan

Teotihuacán, an abandoned ancient city dominated by the massive temples of the sun and the moon. Beyond the city, across a broad valley, lay the Tlaxcalans' mountain home and safety. Cortés's troops marched past the looming temples, encouraged by the thought of friendly territory. As they climbed the hills toward Tlaxcala, they left behind the plains known to the Indians as Micoatl—the Path of the Dead.

Suddenly scouts arrived and breathlessly told Cortés the main Aztec army lay ahead of them. Reaching the heights overlooking the Valley of Otumba, the Spaniards beheld an Aztec army two hundred thousand strong. Warriors in quilted cotton armor formed a white wall blocking the Spaniards' path to Tlaxcala. With icy calm, Cortés instructed his men. They were to advance, thrusting with their swords and lances, taking special care to kill the leaders. Calling on God for protection, Cortés ordered his tiny command forward.

The Spaniards and Tlaxcalans quickly found themselves engulfed in a swirling mass of Aztec warriors. Castilian swords felled the Mexicans by the hundreds, but thousands pressed forward to replace them. The battle lasted for hours. Just as it seemed the Aztecs would overwhelm the exhausted Spaniards, Cortés saw the enemy commander, Cihuaca, bright in his feathered robes, held aloft on a litter. Above the roar of battle, the captain-general shouted to four of his trusted lieutenants to follow him, and together they charged the Aztec leader. The desperate riders tore through the enemy ranks, slashing and trampling the bronze warriors. Cortés drove his lance through Cihuaca, toppling him from the litter, snatched the chieftain's feathered banner, and held it triumphantly above his head.

The Battle of Otumba

Hernando Cortés's decision to attack the enemy commander during the Battle of Otumba turned what could have been a Spanish defeat into an Aztec disaster. Bernal Díaz in his Discovery and Conquest of Mexico: 1517–1521 *recounts the critical moment.*

"[The Aztecs] killed and wounded a great number of our soldiers, but it pleased God that Cortés and [his] Captains . . . who went in his Company reached the place where the Captain General of the Mexicans was marching with his banner displayed, and with rich golden armour and great gold and silver plumes. When Cortés saw him with many other Mexican Chieftains all wearing great plumes, he said to our Captains: 'Now, Senores, let us break through them and leave none of them unwounded'; and commending themselves to God . . . [they] charged, and Cortés struck his horse against the Mexican Captain, which made him drop his banner, and the rest of our Captains succeeded in breaking through the squadron."

An Aztec Disaster

Panic swept through the Aztec army. Warriors seeing another of Cortés's miracles fled their slain leader and spread despair to their comrades. Seeing victory in reach, Spaniard and Tlaxcalan alike massacred their fleeing enemies. According to Gómara's biography of Cortés, the tide of battle turned with stunning suddenness:

> When the Indians saw their standard and its bearer fall, they dropped their banners to the ground and fled, for such is their custom in war when their general is killed and their standard knocked down. Our men took heart at this and our horse [cavalry] pursued the enemy, slaying an infinity of them, so many, it was said, that I do not venture to guess the exact number. . . . Never had there been a more notable feat of arms in the Indies.[33]

Following the battle, the Spaniards straggled into Tlaxcala without further Aztec interference. Some soldiers feared

A conquistador slays Aztec warriors during the Battle of Otumba. Cortés's skillful planning allowed his soldiers to win in spite of overwhelming odds.

Cortés's Indian allies help him rebuild his forces and replenish his supplies for a renewed assault on the Aztecs.

that the mountain people, seeing the soldiers' condition, might turn on them. Instead, the Tlaxcalans treated the Spaniards as friends and brothers, supplying food and refuge while the battered army rested. Having narrowly escaped with their lives, many soldiers begged Cortés to build ships and return to Cuba as quickly as possible. They should have known better. From the moment the Spaniards entered Tlaxcala, the captain-general began planning his campaign to retake Tenochtitlán. In a passionate speech, Cortés persuaded his men to return to the capital and avenge themselves against the Aztecs.

As the Spaniards recovered from their wounds, reinforcements and supplies arrived from Cuba and Hispaniola through Villa Rica. During the fall of 1520, Cortés's command swelled to nine hundred soldiers equipped with muskets and cannon. Tlaxcalan laborers supervised by the con-

quistadors built twelve brigantines, which were to be transported in sections to Lake Texcoco and there assembled for the assault on Tenochtitlán. As he prepared for war, Cortés sent messengers to Montezuma's young successor, Cuauhtemoc, warning him to disarm and make peace or suffer the consequences. In the meantime, combined Spanish-Tlaxcalan detachments raided towns loyal to the Aztecs. One by one, they fell under Spanish control, but the conquistadors were merely nibbling at their prey. The real blow was yet to come.

Tightening the Grip on Tenochitlán

When Cortés led his men back to the Valley of Mexico in December 1520, two hundred thousand Indian allies marched with him. Generations of Aztec kings had

The Siege of Tenochtitlán Draws to a Close

Toward the end of the siege of Tenochtitlán, the Spaniards pushed the remaining Aztecs into a tiny fraction of the city's total area. According to Gómara in this excerpt from Cortés: The Life of the Conqueror *during the final days of fighting some Aztecs approached Cortés with a pathetic request.*

"The Mexicans, bewailing their ill luck, begged the Spaniards to kill them and have done with it, but certain gentlemen summoned Cortés, who hurried to them, thinking they might be seeking an arrangement [truce]. . . . They said to him: 'Ah, Captain Cortés, since you are a child of the Sun, why do you not persuade him to finish us? O Sun . . . kill us now and relieve us of this long and dreadful penance, for we desire to rest with Quetzalcoatl, who awaits us.' Then they wept and invoked their gods with loud cries. Cortés answered with whatever came to his mind, but could not persuade them. Our Spaniards were struck with pity."

Cortés battles the odds during the siege of Tenochtitlán.

through their abuses and oppression sealed their own fate. Methodically, the allied army seized control of the cities in the valley. Most of the water surrounding the capital was unsuitable for drinking, so Cortés ordered the stone aqueducts that supplied Tenochtitlán's fresh water destroyed. Soon the Spanish brigantines drove Aztec boat traffic from the lake, cutting off the city's food supply. Now the capital's inhabitants faced thirst and starvation. Gradually, Cortés's army tightened its grip on Tenochtitlán.

Trapped on their island fortress, surrounded by the Europeans and the Indians who had once been their subjects, the Aztecs anticipated the siege with complete confidence. Daily, Huitzilopochtli's priests promised Cuauhtemoc that the Aztecs and their gods would soon feast on their enemies' flesh. Encouraged by the war god's prophecies, the Aztecs fought courageously and ingeniously. The conquistadors found their enemy carrying spears tipped with Spanish swords captured during the Noche Triste. Using these and their obsidian-edged swords, Aztec warriors held their ground when charged by cavalry and killed the Spaniards' horses. Retreating warriors often lured the conquistadors into ambushes deep inside the capital. One Aztec trap succeeded so completely that dozens of conquistadors and hundreds of Indian allies died or fell into enemy hands. That night fires burned brightly atop the great pyramid, and the sound of the Aztecs' huge sacrificial drum throbbed across the lake. The conquistadors watched the priests of Huitzilopochtli sacrifice their captured friends to the idols of Mexico.

Despite occasional successes, time was working against the Aztecs. Spanish brigantines kept canoes from supplying the capital with food. In desperation, Tenochtitlán's starving citizens gnawed tree bark and roots. Fresh water proved impossible to find in adequate amounts, leaving the Indians to drink from a few shallow wells and stagnant pools. Still worse for the Aztecs, the Spaniards had left a hidden ally within the capital's walls. One of Narváez's men had carried smallpox, a disease previously unknown in North America, into Tenochtitlán. With no immunities to the disease, the Aztecs died by the thousands .

Reduced to Smoldering Ruins

As the conquistadors advanced into the city, they saw gaunt bodies scattered throughout the streets. Nearly two months into the siege, Cortés invited Cuauhtemoc to surrender and save both his people and their capital, but the young king defiantly refused. Determined swiftly to end the siege, Cortés reluctantly ordered his men to destroy the city as they advanced. If the Aztecs would not surrender the city, the Spaniards would destroy it around them.

Indian farmers with hoes and digging sticks now accompanied the army as it occupied the capital. Soldiers burned and demolished the buildings as they fell under their control, while the Indian allies filled the canals with rubble. Instead of raiding and evacuating the city each day, the conquistadors now occupied all territory gained in the fighting. As the surviving Aztecs crowded into a tiny fraction of the city's area, their suffering increased. Cortés climbed to the summit of a tower and surveyed the scene. Behind him lay the smoldering ruins of the place he had once called the most beautiful city on earth. Beyond the Spanish lines he saw the starving, disease-ridden Aztecs, miserable but defiant, awaiting their fate, and he felt pity for the people he intended to destroy.

In the end, even Cuauhtemoc abandoned all hope of driving the Spaniards from Mexico. Leaving Tenochtitlán to its fate, on August 13 the young monarch boarded a large canoe and tried to slip past Cortés's prowling brigantines to the

Unlike his predecessor Montezuma, Cuauhtemoc bravely fought the Spaniards. Once caught by Cortés, Cuauhtemoc begged the conquistador to kill him.

mainland. An alert Spanish ship captain named Garci Holguín intercepted the vessel, captured Cuauhtemoc, and delivered him to Cortés. Undaunted, the Aztec king urged the captain-general to kill him. In his biography of the conqueror, Gómara describes the encounter:

> [Cortés] received him with royal honors, saluted him cordially, and had him brought near, whereupon Cuauhtemoc touched Cortés' dagger and said: "I have done everything in my power to defend myself and my people. . . . You may do with me whatever you wish, so kill me, for that will be best."[34]

Moved by compassion or practicality, Cortés assured Cuauhtemoc that he would not only spare his life but that he would still allow him to rule his people. At Cortés's command, the last of the Aztec kings climbed to a rooftop and ordered his remaining warriors to lay down their arms. Over seventy thousand surrendered.

The End of the Aztec Empire

Jubilant shouts arose from the Tlaxcalans. Despite Cortés's orders to spare the captives, the fierce mountain warriors ravaged the city and took revenge on their ancient enemies. By nightfall the allies' fury had spent itself, and a drizzling rain covered the dying city. Conqueror and conquered alike took refuge in abandoned buildings as the storm gained strength and pounded the valley. Daybreak brought the grim work of cleansing the city. Crews collected the dead, burying them quickly to avoid the spread of disease, while

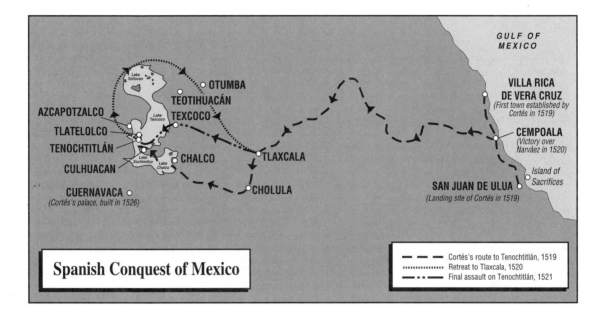

Spanish Conquest of Mexico

GULF OF MEXICO

VILLA RICA DE VERA CRUZ
(First town established by Cortés in 1519)

CEMPOALA
(Victory over Narváez in 1520)

Island of Sacrifices

SAN JUAN DE ULUA
(Landing site of Cortés in 1519)

OTUMBA
TEOTIHUACÁN
TEXCOCO
AZCAPOTZALCO
TLATELOLCO
TENOCHTITLÁN
CULHUACAN
CHALCO
TLAXCALA
CUERNAVACA
(Cortés's palace, built in 1526)
CHOLULA

Lake Xaltocan
Lake Texcoco
Lake Xochimilco
Lake Chalco

- - - - - Cortés's route to Tenochtitlán, 1519
· · · · · · · Retreat to Tlaxcala, 1520
— · — · — Final assault on Tenochtitlán, 1521

Spaniards and their allies set fire to the houses in the precincts where the plague was worst. Quietly, the once proud Aztecs filed past the victors and across the causeways to the mainland, refugees in the land of their ancestors. Behind them smoke rose from what had been the mightiest city in America, carrying the stench of burning flesh skyward. This time no Aztec gods took pleasure in the smell.

8 New Spain of the Ocean Sea

From an Indian point of view, Hernando Cortés was the new ruler of the Aztec realms. The people of Mexico might embrace him as a liberator or fear him as a conqueror, but none could doubt his power. News that the Spaniards had conquered the mightiest people in America flashed like lightning throughout the land. If the white men could subdue the hated Aztecs, who could stand against them? A steady procession of Indian caciques presented themselves to Cortés, offering allegiance to him and to his king across the sea. The reins of power, once held by the Aztec kings, now rested in Cortés's hands.

Unfortunately for the captain-general, his authority rested on less certain grounds in the eyes of Charles I. His right to conquer Mexico depended on permission granted by the council of Villa Rica de Vera Cruz, a legal trick Cortés had used to free himself from Diego Velázquez's control. Enraged that he had been denied the fruits of New Spain's conquest, Velázquez campaigned tirelessly to discredit Cortés with the Crown. Eventually, Cortés had persuaded Charles I to name him governor of New Spain, but the issue remained unsettled.

Cortés's brilliant success excited his competitors' jealousy, and they continued

Ironically, Cortés was never allowed to participate in the settlement of the land he conquered in the name of Spain.

to charge him with crimes, including rebellion against the Crown. Velázquez and his supporters also kept alive rumors that the captain-general had hidden Montezuma's treasure for his own use. In 1526, Charles I sent Luis Pónce de León to investigate the charges against Cortés. Pónce de León immediately stripped Cortés of his governorship. Determined to prove his innocence and reinforce his authority, Cortés sailed for Spain in 1528. There he appealed directly to the king. Accompanied by Aztec nobles, Cortés lavished rich gifts on Charles and dazzled Spain with the wonders of its newest conquest. While all this pleased the king, Charles decided that it was time to rein in his independently minded vassal. He sidestepped Cortés's request to be restored to the governorship, instead declaring him captain-general and Marquess of the Valley of Oaxaca. In effect, Cortés held the power to conquer new lands and gained title to an estate the equal of some European kingdoms. With his great wealth, he launched fruitless expeditions to search for mythical golden kingdoms west of Mexico. Otherwise, he remained on the sidelines in the land he had conquered. A string of officials appointed by the king would complete the task of developing and ruling New Spain.

Tenochtitlán Is Rebuilt as Mexico City

Long before Charles stripped Cortés of his authority, the conqueror began molding Mexico into New Spain of the Ocean Sea. No longer an Indian empire, it would be a Spanish colony and its people would adopt Spanish ways. Cortés envisioned a populous Spanish city replacing the Aztec capital. Tenochtitlán, the soul and symbol of Aztec power in Mexico, lay flattened by months of siege. Tens of thousands of Indian laborers supervised by the conquistadors began building Mexico City on its ruins. Stones torn from temples, palaces, and dwellings rose again to form a church and homes for the conquistadors. With a shrewd sense of symbolism, Cortés ordered his home built on the site once occupied by Montezuma's palace. So lavish was the captain-general's residence that his critics claimed its construction had consumed whole forests of cedar.

Lumber was not the only commodity consumed by the ambitious building project. Hundreds of Indians died from hunger, disease, and exhaustion each day in Mexico City's construction. The siege of Tenochtitlán had taken place when the valley's farmers normally tilled their soil. Crops that had been planted were neglected or devoured by hundreds of thousands of foraging warriors. Now food shortages combined with the demands of heavy labor brought starvation to Indian workers. If Gómara portrayed the situation accurately, the Indians accepted the task and its risks voluntarily and cheerfully.

> Upon hearing that Mexico-Tenochtitlán was being rebuilt . . . so many people came that there was hardly room for them to stand for a league roundabout. They worked so hard and ate so little that they sickened, the pestilence attacked them, and an infinite number died. . . . Nevertheless, their songs and music . . . and their exchanges of pleasantries were something to hear. . . . Little by little, they rebuilt Mexico, with 100,000 houses better than the old ones . . . after our fashion.[35]

Mexico City included a precinct to be occupied only by Spanish settlers, but the conquistadors would not long remain there. The Spaniards had come to Mexico to make their fortunes, especially to find treasure. By the time Cortés set aside King Charles's and his own shares of Aztec booty, too little remained to make the conquistadors rich. They now realized their only hope for wealth lay in obtaining land grants. Given the Spaniards' small numbers, their dislike of manual labor, and the vastness of the land, it would take Indian workers to produce Spanish wealth. Even so, the captain-general understood that granting *encomiendas* to his men endangered both the Indians' lives and the colony's success.

Under the *encomienda* system, the king allowed subjects he wished to reward Indian labor in a specific area of a colony. In return, the recipient (the *encomendero*) of the grant was to give the Indians spiritual guidance and insure that they became Catholics. The Spanish monarchs had intended this system to give colonists a source of income from newly conquered lands. At the same time, the *encomendero* was supposed to protect the natives under his care from abuse. Although the system often did not protect the natives, Cortés believed it was necessary to grant *encomiendas* in New Spain.

From the beginning of the conquest, Cortés sought to make Spanish rule in New Spain more humane and enlightened than it had been in Hispaniola and Cuba. Even a warrior so fierce as Cortés realized that dead Indians could not work, and without Indian workers the Spaniards

Mexico City in the sixteenth century. The bustling European-style city was built on the ruins of Tenochtitlán.

Cortés Grants *Encomiendas*

Although Cortés at first opposed encomiendas, *he surrendered to his men's demands that he grant them. In this excerpt from* The Encomienda in New Spain, *historian Lesley Byrd Simpson outlines Cortés's reasoning.*

"[Cortés] had spent twenty years in the islands and had witnessed the disastrous effect of the Spanish occupation upon the natives there. He, like many enlightened men of the time, believed that the destruction was chargeable to the encomienda, and he resolved that the evil was not to be introduced into the new lands. . . .

At the fall of Mexico City, Cortés had with him some 1,500 men who were under the most shadowy military obligation to their chief. . . . They had fought hard and suffered severely in the Mexican campaign. They had received no pay for two years except the small amount of booty left after Cortés had withheld his own not inconsiderable share and had sent a like amount to the [king]. . . . There was no reward for them but Indians, and Indians they must and would have. Cortés was too accomplished a statesman to allow principles to stand in the way of expedience and yielded to the threatening insistence of his men."

could not build a prosperous colony. With the Caribbean experience fresh in his mind, Cortés at first urged Charles I to outlaw the *encomienda* in New Spain. The captain-general soon set aside his objections to *encomiendas* when his soldiers, denied what they considered a fair share of the spoils won after three years of hard fighting, insisted on payment. Although *encomiendas* were outlawed by Charles I in 1520, Cortés, anxious to avoid rebellion among his own men, granted *encomiendas* soon after the fall of Tenochtitlán. The captain-general now insisted the grants were essential to building the new colony and paying the costs of its military occupation. The king, fearing chaos if he revoked the *encomiendas* and unwilling to pay for colonial expenses out of the royal treasury, accepted the situation. The conquistadors could keep their grants but would not be allowed to pass them on to their heirs. Despite Cortés's and Charles I's best intentions, many of the evils associated with the *encomienda* in the Caribbean invaded New Spain.

The evils soon became obvious. Although Cortés rewarded his faithful Tlaxcalan allies by decreeing that they should not be enslaved, countless other Indians were forced into servitude. Despite the Spanish monarch's intention that the *encomienda* be used to protect the natives, many found themselves slaves in fact if

Indians are enslaved in the mines under the Spanish encomienda *system.*

not in law. Not surprisingly, many of the conquistadors who had witnessed the natives' mass human sacrifices now considered the Indians beasts unfit to join the family of God. If this were true, the settlers could justify using them for both profit and pleasure.

Some colonists formed raiding parties and ranged far and wide, abducting Indians and selling them into slavery. Conditions became even worse in 1528 when Charles I placed New Spain under the control of the first *audiencia*, a council headed by Nuno de Guzmán. Guzmán stole Indian lands, permitted the settlers to rape native women, and enslaved thousands of natives for his own profit. So vicious was Guzmán's rule that some Indians reportedly decided not to bear children as long as he held power in Mexico. However, if some Spaniards brought misery to the natives, others did their best to defend them.

The Catholic Church Defends the Indians

Surely the greatest defender of New Spain's natives during early colonial times was the Franciscan Juan de Zumarraga, who served as Mexico's first bishop. Already sixty years old when he arrived, Zumarraga zealously protected his flock. The bishop arrived in Mexico just as Nuno de Guzmán began his reign of terror. Zumarraga sympathized with the natives' suffering but lacked the power to stop Guzmán's abuses. Realizing Guzmán would permit no interference in his policies, the bishop secretly sent a message to Charles I. Zumarraga entrusted the letter to a sailor who encased it in a ball of wax and concealed it in a barrel of oil bound for Spain. In the letter, Zumarraga condemned Guzmán's misrule and boldly instructed Charles I to repent if he had approved the abusive policies. To his credit, the king replaced Guzmán and considered reforms to help his new subjects.

During his years as Mexico's bishop, Zumarraga also founded academies to educate Aztec boys and girls. In 1537, he imported what may have been America's first printing press. He saw to it that books were produced to help educate both Spanish and Indian students. Some settlers grumbled that the bishop opposed branding Indians and using them as pack animals. The natives rightly viewed Zumarraga as their protector and brought their complaints about Spanish mistreatment to him. When death ended his service to the church in Mexico in 1548, he enjoyed the affection and respect of Indian and Spaniard alike.

Other churchmen also championed the Indians' cause. A Franciscan, Toribio de Motolina, challenged the abuses of the *encomienda* system. Yet another Franciscan, the Flemish Pedro de Gante, established a school for Indian boys near Mexico City. As bishop of Michoacán, Vasco de Quiroga established utopian villages to protect the natives from abduction by slave hunters. Here the Indians shared the fruits of their labor and lived under the church's guidance.

Although they did not know it, the natives also had defenders in Europe. Debate

The Spanish Church in America

Spanish churchmen devoted their lives to bringing Spain's new colonial subjects into the Catholic Church. In this passage extracted from A History of Latin America from the Beginnings to the Present, *Hubert Herring portrays the Spanish church's missionary zeal.*

"The priests who came with the conquerors were afire with the crusading zeal of a Spain which had rid itself of unbelieving Moslems and Jews and had gone far in cleansing itself of timeserving priests. . . . As colonizers followed conquerors, the Church in America was influenced by Charles I's battles for the faith, waged in his international role as Charles V [Holy Roman Emperor]—battles against the Moslems in Africa, against France in league with the Turks, and against the Protestant powers of northern Europe. . . . This spiritual climate gave zest to the friars who were pouring out their energy and devotion upon the hard frontier of America. However, after the sixteenth century, religious devotion lessened both in Spain and America. . . . The Church became rich in land and gold. The many noble-hearted priests were outnumbered by those who found America comfortable and secure."

raged in both the colonies and Spain as to the spiritual nature of the Indians. During her reign Isabella had declared the Indians free citizens of the Spanish empire. In 1537, Pope Paul III decreed that the Indians retained the rights to their own property and were not to be enslaved. Following Pope Paul's lead, Charles I forbade the enslavement of Indians and declared them free vassals of the Crown. Unfortunately, the Crown did not consistently protect native rights. In 1545, Charles I revoked his earlier promise of freedom to the Indians and declared that the conquerors could hand down *encomiendas* to their heirs. Now many of

Charles I was inconsistent in his attitudes toward the Indians, at one time protecting their rights and later revoking those same protections.

those Indians who had remained free often became peasants working on estates granted to the conquerors.

Natives Embrace Catholicism

In the end, the Indians' advocates and exploiters both enjoyed some measure of success. The natives, already comfortable with religious ritual, embraced Catholicism by the millions. Thanks to the churchmen's efforts, many natives learned Latin before they learned Spanish, and on occasion so many Indians joined the church that priests practiced mass baptisms. Often the Indian tendency, sometimes encouraged by priests, to blend the old religions with the new made the transition easier. Old gods became identified with saints and continued to receive veneration. A Catholic church was built atop the pyramid at Cholula, and smoke from incense once burned to please the gods now rose in the church sanctuary.

In the end, the churchmen could save the Indians' souls but could not always protect their bodies. The natives continued to be exploited by their new Spanish masters. After the conquest, Indian labor produced both native and European crops in New Spain's fields. Indian workers tended cattle, sheep, horses, and hogs imported from Spain. The silver and gold that filled the holds of the treasure ships bound for Spain were mined by Indians. Once the people of Mexico had served the Aztecs and their gods. Now they served the Spaniards and their God.

Mexico Transformed

It was inevitable that the conquistadors and the people they conquered would make a new people and a new land of Mexico. Life in a land four thousand miles from Spain among a people who outnumbered them brought about changes the conquerors did not expect, including changes in Spain itself. Life as subjects of the growing Spanish empire altered the Mexicans and their land in ways they could never have foreseen. The cost was high.

Lives Lost and Saved Due to the Conquest

Although an accurate accounting is impossible, millions of Indians died because of the conquest. Combat with the Spaniards killed tens of thousands. According to Gómara's account, over twelve thousand died in a single day at the end of Tenochtitlán's siege. Estimates of Mexico's population at the time of the conquest vary widely from eleven million to twenty-five million. Over half died during the first smallpox outbreak. According to Dr. Frederick F. Cartwright:

Within a space of less than six months hardly one village remained uninfected in the known regions of New Spain. The mortality was appalling. . . . When Cortés entered the city [Tenochtitlán] he found that nearly half of the inhabitants had succumbed to the infection. The same rate of mortality was general throughout New Spain.[36]

By the end of the sixteenth century, measles and mumps, combined with famine following the siege, added to the toll, but smallpox proved the greatest curse. Once a relatively mild childhood disease, it seems to have changed and returned to Europe in a more deadly form. By the eighteenth century, the new strain had spread as far as Australia. Apparently, the introduction of smallpox into Mexico triggered a string of devastating worldwide epidemics.

Although we may never know how many died because of the Spaniards' arrival in Mexico, we do know the conquistadors stopped the slaughter of sacrificial victims. By the time of the conquest, Indians throughout the region practiced human sacrifice, but the Aztecs had converted their empire into a killing machine. Estimates of the victims killed to dedicate the great temple in Tenochtitlán range from as few as ten thousand to as many as eighty

Smallpox Comes to Mexico

In the General History of the Things of New Spain, *translated from Aztec texts by Fray Bernardino de Sahagún, the people of Mexico left their impressions of the plague that resulted from an outbreak of smallpox.*

"Before the Spaniards had risen against us, first there came to be prevalent a great sickness, a plague. . . . There spread over the people a great destruction of men. Some it indeed covered [with pustules]; they were spread everywhere, on one's face, on one's head, on one's breast. . . . There was indeed perishing; many indeed died of it. No longer could they walk; they only lay in their . . . beds. No longer could they move, no longer could they bestir themselves, no longer could they raise themselves. . . . And when they bestirred themselves, much did they cry out. There was much perishing. . . . Many just died of hunger. . . . There was no one to take care of another; there was no one to attend to another."

thousand. As the Aztecs expanded their empire, more potential victims fell into their hands. And as the Aztecs and their kings gained more power, their obsession with feeding the gods also grew. Despite

Tenochtitlán's exotic beauty and the Aztecs' impressive achievements, by 1519 it had become the capital of an empire based on large-scale ritual cannibalism. The conquistadors halted an ever expanding blood-

Natives are baptized into the Catholic faith by Spanish priests. Catholic missionaries were tremendously successful in converting large numbers of Indians.

bath in Mexico. Is it any wonder both the Aztecs' subjects and neighbors joined the Spaniards in the conquest?

The Spaniards so closely identified Aztec culture with idolatry and ritual butchery that they did their best to eliminate it. For centuries, the Spanish people had dedicated themselves to cleansing their homeland of pagan influence, and the conquistadors considered Indian religion devil worship. Not surprisingly, few Aztec or Mayan books with their pictographic writings survived the conquest. Priests educated Indian children in ways designed to make them better Catholics and subjects of the empire. While some Spaniards, such as Bernardino de Sahagún, labored heroically to preserve Aztec history, by the end of the sixteenth century Aztec culture remained only a vague memory in the land that gave it birth.

A Blended People

A new culture, a hybrid of things Indian and Spanish, replaced the old. Mexico's religion serves as an example. In December 1531, an Indian named Juan Diego reported to Bishop Zumarraga that the Virgin Mary had appeared to him just outside Mexico City near the hill of Tepeyac. Unlike Spanish impressions of the mother of Jesus, this woman was bronze skinned and black haired. Breathlessly, Diego told Zumarraga that the Virgin had said she was the mother of all Indians and that she wanted a shrine built where she stood. The bishop listened intently but refused to accept the miracle.

Twice more Diego returned claiming to have seen the Virgin at the same location.

Our Lady of Guadalupe, the patron saint of the Indians of Mexico.

On the third occasion, he said roses miraculously sprang from the ground on the hillside. Wrapping the flowers in his cloak as proof of the Virgin's return, he hurried to the bishop. When Diego opened the cloth, the roses had disappeared, but an image of Mary as an Indian woman remained on the cloak. The portrait now hangs above the altar in the church built near Tepeyac honoring Our Lady of Guadalupe. While this story may arouse skepticism among non-Catholics, Diego's vision brought an important message to the people of Mexico—the Catholic faith belonged as much to the Indians as it did to their Spanish conquerors. The two peoples were becoming one.

Because of the conquest, Mexico's people officially follow one faith, but Mexican worship blends European and Indian traditions. Over 95 percent of the population is Catholic, but Indian ways have influenced the church. The church dedicated to Our Lady of Guadalupe, the mother of the Indians, was built on a site long identified with the goddess Tonantzin, known to the Aztecs as Our Mother. Indian influence is even more pronounced in southern Mexico. There, worshipers still kneel at the feet of ancient idols once used in the Indians' native religions. Now the statues are called by the names of the saints.

Despite this union of the two religions, many Mexicans still resent the Catholic Church as a symbol of things Spanish. When Mexico adopted its new constitution in 1917, the document imposed severe restrictions on the church, that most Spanish of Mexican institutions. Church lands were confiscated, the number of priests was limited, and priests were denied the right to vote or hold public office. For much of Mexico's national existence, politicians have gained favor with the people by condemning the church. Mexico's mixed religion seems an uneasy compromise between the old and the new.

Just as Mexico's religion became a mixture of the old and the new, so did the people. From the beginning, Indian caciques offered their daughters to the conquistadors, who gladly took them as wives and mistresses. Even Cortés, who was married before he left Cuba, fathered at least two children by Indian women, including one of Montezuma's daughters.

His oldest son and heir to his estate, Martin, was born to Marina. Today, less than 10 percent of Mexico's people are classified as white. Nearly 30 percent are Indians, and the remainder are mestizos.

Although most of the population has become a blend of Spaniard and Indian, much Spanish influence survives. Spanish language, architecture, and customs prevail throughout Mexico. For generations Mexicans admired and followed strong-willed dictators, the caudillos, whose greed, ambition, and lust for power are reminiscent of Cortés and his lieutenants. Eventually the ways those men divided conquered land may have dramatically affected both Mexico's and Spain's economies.

The Conquest's Economic Impact

Many Mexicans are desperately poor. It seems likely that Spanish colonization policies contributed to the poverty that has haunted Mexico for centuries. The *encomienda* system left huge estates in the hands of the few. For much of its history, Mexico has been plagued by the resentment of the poor and landless people against the great estate holders. For all the land's great potential wealth, today the average Mexican's income is only one-seventh that of a U.S. citizen's. For centuries, rebel leaders in Mexico have attracted followers by promising to take land from the rich and give it to the poor.

Despite Mexico's poverty, for a time the Spanish lust for precious metals created prosperity. Gold and silver enticed settlers to New Spain who mined more

The Catholic Church in Mexico

More than any other factor in the conquest, the Catholic Church molded Mexico into the new country it would become. According to historian J. Fred Rippy, in this passage from Latin America: A Modern History, *from the beginning the church was a powerful force for good.*

"There was no more important institution . . . than the Roman Catholic Church. To it early Spanish American society owed much that was beneficial and little that was harmful. . . . If the intolerant zeal of a few had sometimes abetted the cruelties of the conquerors, if eagerness to enlarge the wealth of the church had led some to make use of compulsory Indian labor, the tender human sympathy of others had often restrained ruthless laymen and softened the hard lot of the natives. . . . If there was just ground for complaint at the accumulation of ecclesiastical wealth, it must be admitted that the colonial inhabitants owed to the church nearly all that they received in education, hospitalization, and charity."

A nineteenth-century painting depicts a rural Catholic church in Mexico.

bullion in fifty years than the Indians had found in centuries. Boomtowns sprang up around the mines, and the demand for farm produce to supply the miners' needs increased. The mining industry triggered expanded trade and the creation of countless businesses large and small. As the owner of all Mexican mines, the Crown, anxious to obtain its Royal Fifth of the proceeds, strictly regulated the mining industry and encouraged its development. Although smuggling made an accurate accounting difficult, by the beginning of the nineteenth century Spain may have extracted nine billion dollars in gold and silver from Mexico alone.

Spain's success in finding treasure made her a target and enriched her enemies. French and English privateers and pirates constantly preyed on the Spanish treasure convoys from the New World. In addition to that diverted to France and England, untold amounts simply went to the bottom of the Caribbean, sunk by privateer attacks or storms. In 1687, an Englishman named William Phips salvaged twenty-six tons of silver from a Spanish wreck. In 1715 and 1733 two hurricanes sank thirty treasure ships near the Bahamas. Today modern salvage crews still search for the wrecks of Spanish treasure galleons.

Spain's colonial wealth made her the envy of her rivals, England and France, but the New World's riches proved a mixed blessing to the mother country. Instead of using her New World bullion to build a solid industrial and agricultural base at home, Spain's kings lavished their

I Am the King!

While traveling through Mexico, author Gene S. Stuart encountered a remarkable example of Mexican pride in its Aztec past. This passage from his book The Mighty Aztecs *describes the incident.*

"In [the] gardens at Texcotzingo, I found a youthful appreciation of [Aztec] heritage. . . . As I sat on steps leading down to the ruler's seat, four young schoolboys—the oldest no more than 12—came running and laughing down the path. One boy stopped suddenly. . . . He became lost in thought as the others ran on ahead. He turned to me. . . .

He proclaimed—'I am the king!' 'You?' I asked. 'Yes.' With conscious dignity he seated himself on the ancient throne. He leaned forward, his chin cupped in one hand, and looked out at the valley below us, the mountains around. He spread his arms wide. 'I am Cuauhtemoc and these lands are mine!' he shouted. Content, he leaned back and gazed at his domain. Then he was off with a wave, running, laughing, climbing to join his companions. Ascending."

resources on wars in Europe. Gold and silver hired mercenaries and built fleets while Spanish farms declined. Spanish consumers bought foreign goods since few were produced in Spain itself. The torrent of bullion caused inflation in Spain and, to a lesser extent, in Europe, an event sometimes called the price revolution. In the end, Spain gained few long-term benefits from New World riches. As historian Charles E. Chapman observes:

> Spain wasted her energies and expended her wealth in a fruitless attempt . . . to become the dominant power in Europe. . . . What she took from the Americas with the one hand, she squandered in Europe with the other.[37]

Spain's neglected economy stagnated, and her once proud military fell behind those of England and France. By the seventeenth and eighteenth centuries, Spain was heavily in debt to Europe's great banking houses. Weakened and overextended, Spain lost most of her American colonies early in the nineteenth century. The glory of imperial Spain continued to fade for generations.

Two Worlds Become One

In Mexico, the dim images of two great empires remain. Tourists attend bullfights, which are enthusiastically announced in Spanish. Between bullfights Indian dancers clad in bright feathered garments whirl about as their ancestors did before the Spaniards reached Mexico. Cathedrals built on Spanish designs rise above the Mexican landscape while nearby brilliant murals cover tall buildings as they did in Tenochtitlán. From time to time, Mexican workmen excavate Mexico City's streets to lay new pipelines. Sometimes they strike stone and discover the steps of an Aztec temple or an idol buried when Cortés built his capital on the ruins of Montezuma's. The new Mexico rests on the debris of the old.

Notes

Introduction: When Cultures Collide

1. Hubert Herring, *A History of Latin America from the Beginnings to the Present.* New York: Alfred A. Knopf, 1972, p. 49.

Chapter 1: Toward the Setting Sun

2. Bernal Díaz del Castillo, *The Discovery and Conquest of Mexico: 1517–1521.* A. P. Maudslay, trans. New York: Farrar, Straus, and Cudahy, 1956, p. 4.
3. Díaz, *The Discovery and Conquest,* p. 9.
4. Díaz, *The Discovery and Conquest,* p. 10.
5. Díaz, *The Discovery and Conquest,* p. 12.
6. Díaz, *The Discovery and Conquest,* p. 13.
7. Díaz, *The Discovery and Conquest,* p. 13.

Chapter 2: The Grijalva Expedition

8. Díaz, *The Discovery and Conquest,* p. 24.
9. Díaz, *The Discovery and Conquest,* p. 28.
10. Díaz, *The Discovery and Conquest,* p. 28.
11. Francisco López de Gómara, *Cortés: The Life of the Conqueror.* Lesley Byrd Simpson, trans. and ed. Los Angeles: University of California Press, 1964, pp. 14, 15.

Chapter 3: "I Came to Get Gold!"

12. Wallace K. Ferguson, *Europe in Transition: 1300–1520.* Boston: Houghton Mifflin, 1962, pp. 464–65.
13. William H. Prescott, *Conquest of Mexico.* New York: The Book League of America, 1934, p. 15.
14. Bernal Díaz, *The Conquest of New Spain.* J. M. Cohen, trans. New York: Penguin Classics, 1976, p. 45.
15. Quoted in Díaz, *Conquest,* p. 46.
16. Quoted in Díaz, *Conquest,* p. 46.

Chapter 4: The Return to Yucatán

17. Gómara, *Cortés,* p. 31.
18. Hernando Cortés, *Hernan Cortés: Letters from Mexico.* A. R. Pagden, trans. New York: Grossman Publishers, 1971, p. 18.
19. Díaz, *Conquest,* p. 69.
20. Díaz, *Conquest,* p. 70.
21. Díaz, *Conquest,* p. 87.
22. Gómara, *Cortés,* pp. 49–50.

Chapter 5: "Deeds So Marvellous"

23. Gómara, *Cortés,* p. 74.
24. Díaz, *The Discovery and Conquest,* pp. 92, 93.
25. Díaz, *The Discovery and Conquest,* p. 119.

Chapter 6: "I Am He"

26. Díaz, *The Discovery and Conquest,* p. 187.
27. Bernardino de Sahagún, *General History of the Things of New Spain.* Arthur J. O. Anderson and Charles E. Dibble, trans. Santa Fe: School of American Research and the University of Utah, Monographs of the School of American Research, 1975, p. 44.
28. Díaz, *The Discovery and Conquest,* p. 230.
29. Díaz, *The Discovery and Conquest,* p. 230.
30. Quoted in Patricia de Fuentes, trans., *The Conquistadors: First-Person Accounts of Mexico.* New York: The Orion Press, 1963, p. 46.
31. Díaz, *The Discovery and Conquest,* p. 295.

Chapter 7: "A Notable Feat of Arms"

32. Prescott, *Conquest,* p. 278.
33. Gómara, *Cortés,* p. 225.
34. Gómara, *Cortés,* p. 292.

Chapter 8: New Spain of the Ocean Sea

35. Gómara, *Cortés,* p. 324.

Epilogue: Mexico Transformed

36. Frederick F. Cartwright, *Disease and History.* New York: New American Library, 1972, p. 119.
37. Charles E. Chapman, *A History of Spain.* New York: Macmillan, 1931, p. 234.

For Further Reading

Author's Note: The following books represent several perspectives on the conquest of Mexico. Most are available in libraries.

Maurice Collis, *Cortés and Montezuma*. New York: Harcourt, Brace and Company, 1954. A biographical work that sheds light on the characters of the conqueror and the conquered, this book is thoroughly researched.

Hernando Cortés, *Hernán Cortés: Letters from Mexico*. A. R. Pagden, trans. New York: Grossman Publishers, 1971. A large work detailing the conquest as Cortés saw it (Cortés sometimes misstates dates).

Bernal Díaz, *The Conquest of New Spain*. J. M. Cohen, trans. New York: Penguin Classics, 1976. The best source on the conquest, this book is a colorful account written by an adventurer who accompanied the first three expeditions to Mexico.

Bernal Díaz del Castillo, *The Discovery and Conquest of Mexico: 1517–1521*. A. P. Maudslay, trans. Farrar, Straus, and Cudahy, 1956. This is the standard translation of the most important source of information about the conquest.

Francisco López de Gómara, *Cortés: The Life of the Conqueror*. Lesley Byrd Simpson, trans. and ed. Los Angeles: University of California Press, 1964. Written by Cortés's secretary years after the conquest, this source portrays Cortés in a more positive light than does Díaz's chronicle.

Paul Horgan, *Conquistadors in North American History*. Greenwich: Fawcett Publications, 1965. Pulitzer Prize–winner Paul Horgan's book on the conquest of North America is one of the most enjoyable works on the subject.

Hammond Innes, *The Conquistadors*. New York: Alfred A. Knopf, 1969. Innes's account describes the conquest against the backdrop of the political situation in Europe.

William Weber Johnson, *Cortés*. Boston: Little, Brown, 1975. Johnson's biography of the conqueror notes the development of Mexican hostility toward the conqueror and things Spanish.

Bartolomé de Las Casas, *The Devastation of the Indies: A Brief Account*. Herme Briffault, trans. Baltimore: The Johns Hopkins University Press, 1992.

———, *History of the Indies*. Andree Collard, trans. New York: Harper & Row, 1971. Las Casas wrote grim descriptions of Spanish mistreatment of the Indians throughout the Caribbean. Although he often exaggerated casualties, his writings did much to convince Europeans the Spanish were mindless brutes in their dealings with the Indians.

Stephen R. Lilley, *The Importance of Hernando Cortés*. San Diego: Lucent Books, 1996. Drawing heavily on contemporary accounts of the conquest and Cortés's letters, this book focuses primarily on Hernando Cortés's impact on the conquest of Mexico.

William H. Prescott, *Conquest of Mexico.* New York: The Book League of America, 1934. A blind scholar writing in the early 1800s, Prescott crafted a beautiful, thorough, and often wordy account of the conquest. This book is still considered one of the best works on the subject.

Bernardino de Sahagún, *General History of the Things of New Spain.* Arthur J. O. Anderson and Charles E. Dibble, trans. Santa Fe: School of American Research and the University of Utah, Monographs of the School of American Research, 1975. A fascinating translation from Aztec writings, this provides an Indian perspective of the conquest. Sometimes the translations are wordy and repetitive.

Lesley Byrd Simpson, *The Encomienda in New Spain: The Beginning of Spanish Mexico.* Los Angeles: University of California Press, 1966. Simpson's book describes legal and organizational problems often ignored by other works on the conquest.

Hugh Thomas, *The Conquest of Mexico.* New York: Simon & Schuster, 1993. The size of Thomas's book, 812 pages, makes it a challenge to read, but it serves as a very complete study of the conquest. Like many earlier historians, Thomas emphasizes the importance of Cortés's leadership in bringing about Spanish victory over the Aztecs.

Victor Wolfgang von Hagen, *The Aztec: Man and Tribe.* New York: New American Library, 1962. Von Hagen's book provides a thorough description of Aztec culture. It also includes an excellent bibliography and a chronology paralleling ancient Indian developments with those in ancient Europe.

Lois Warburton, *Aztec Civilization.* San Diego: Lucent Books, 1995. Warburton's book provides a very compact and readable account of Aztec history and culture.

S. Jeffrey K. Wilkerson, "Following Cortés: Path to Conquest," *National Geographic,* vol. 166, no. 4, October 1984. Wilkerson's article takes the reader on a tour of the conquered land through colorful illustrations.

Works Consulted

Mortimer Adler, ed., *The Annals of America, 1493-1754.* Vol. 1. Chicago: Encyclopedia Britannica, 1968. This multivolume set includes documents pertaining to American history from colonization to the mid–twentieth century.

Maurice Boyd, *Tabascan Myths and Legends.* Fort Worth: Texas Christian University Press, 1969. This little-known work describes the beliefs of the first mainland people the Grijalva and Cortés expeditions encountered.

Caesar C. Cantu, *Cortés and the Fall of the Aztec Empire.* Los Angeles: Modern World Publishing Company, 1966. Cantu's book stresses the role played by the natives in destroying the Aztec empire.

Frederick F. Cartwright, *Disease and History.* New York: New American Library, 1972. A fascinating book dealing with cases where disease has altered world events. The work claims European entry into Mexico caused massive depopulation due to disease.

C. W. Ceram, *Gods, Graves, and Scholars: The Story of American Archaeology.* New York: Bantam Books, 1972. This book contains a brief but very readable summary of Cortés's conquest and does a fine job of describing its importance in world history.

Fernando Cervantes, "The Devil and the Saints in the Conquest of Mexico," *History Today,* April 1994. Cervantes's article argues that similarities between native religions and Roman Catholicism helped bring about the Indians' conversion.

Charles E. Chapman, *A History of Spain.* New York: Macmillan, 1931. Chapman argues that Latin America was destined to become increasingly important economically and politically to the world and that it could be best understood through the Spanish heritage that shaped it.

Geoffrey W. Conrad and Arthur A. Demarest, *Religion and Empire: The Dynamics of Aztec and Inca Expansionism.* Cambridge: Cambridge University Press, 1984. Young readers may find this book difficult, but it is interesting for the authors' argument that the Aztec practice of mass human sacrifice and cannibalism were practical responses to their circumstances.

R. Trevor Davies, *The Golden Century of Spain.* New York: St. Martin's Press, 1967. Davies's well-researched book includes appendixes showing the great wealth in precious metals Spain extracted from her American colonies.

J. H. Elliott, *Imperial Spain: 1469–1716.* New York: St. Martin's Press, 1963. Elliott examines the question of how a country as poor and barren as Spain could so suddenly achieve a world empire and just as suddenly suffer decline.

Wallace K. Ferguson, *Europe in Transition: 1300–1520.* Boston: Houghton Mifflin, 1962. Ferguson's book surveys European history in the time leading up to the conquest.

Patricia de Fuentes, trans., *The Conquistadors: First-Person Accounts of Mexico.* New York: The Orion Press, 1963. Fuentes's collection of eyewitness accounts contains two short but valuable accounts of the conquest.

Peter Hassler, "Cutting Through the Myth of Human Sacrifice: The Lies of the Conquistadors," *World Press Review,* December 1992. Hassler argues that no hard evidence exists that Aztec human sacrifice ever took place. Cortés and his men, therefore, fabricated their horrific accounts to justify the conquest of Mexico.

Hubert Herring, *A History of Latin America from the Beginnings to the Present.* New York: Alfred A. Knopf, 1972. A large work overviewing Latin America from its colonization to the 1970s, Herring's book explains Spanish colonial policies.

Martin A. S. Hume, *Spain: Its Greatness and Decay: 1479–1788.* London: Cambridge University Press, 1931. Hume concludes that Spain wasted its American resources trying to extend its power into central Europe and through unwise economic policies.

William Weber Johnson, *Mexico.* New York: Time Incorporated, 1961. A survey book on Mexican history, this work helps the reader understand the conquest's impact on Mexico.

Benjamin Keen, *The Aztec Image in Western Thought.* New Brunswick, NJ: Rutgers University Press, 1971. A complex and scholarly book not easily understood by young readers, Keen's book explains how Europeans' cultural experiences molded their reaction to Aztec culture.

Francis Clement Kelly, *Blood Drenched Altars: Mexican Study and Comment.* Milwaukee: The Bruce Publishing Company, 1935. As the title indicates, Kelly condemns the Aztec obsession with human sacrifice. It helps the reader understand how each generation views past events in light of their own experiences.

F. A. Kirkpatrick, *The Spanish Conquistadors.* New York: World Publishing Company, 1962. A biographical work, Kirkpatrick's book gives a balanced view of Cortés and his role in the conquest.

Hilde Krueger, *Malinche or Farewell to Myths.* New York: An Arrowhead Press Book for Storm Publishers, 1948. This book deals primarily with Doña Marina and emphasizes the Indian belief that Cortés and his mistress were one god.

Bartolomé de Las Casas, *Tears of the Indians* and *The Life of Las Casas,* Sir Arthur Helps, trans. Williamstown: The John Lilburne Company, Publishers, 1970. Basing his work both on his own observation and on hearsay, Las Casas was perhaps the earliest and harshest critic of Spanish conduct in the Americas. His books represent a lifetime of campaigning for Indian rights.

James Lockhart, *The Nahuas After the Conquest: A Social and Cultural History.* Stanford: Stanford University Press, 1992. Lockhart has written a scholarly account of the impact the conquest had on the people of Mexico.

Bart MacDowell, "The Aztecs," *National Geographic,* vol. 158, no. 6, December 1980. MacDowell's article describes

Aztec culture and history and provides dramatic photographs and paintings of how historians believe the Aztecs appeared at the time of the conquest.

Richard Lee Marks, *Cortés: The Great Adventurer and the Fate of Aztec Mexico*. New York: Alfred A. Knopf, 1993. Marks admits Cortés's darker side but still writes admiringly of the conqueror and his role in the conquest.

Charles L. Mee Jr., "That Fateful Moment When Two Civilizations Came Face to Face," *Smithsonian*, October 1992. Mee's article provides a compact summary of the conquest. Mee argues that the Aztecs' custom of wounding or capturing opponents in warfare combined with the Spaniards' effective use of their steel swords did much to assure Spanish victory.

Michael C. Meyer and William L. Sherman, *The Course of Mexican History*. New York: Oxford University Press, 1979. Meyer and Sherman's work supplies a broader view of Mexico during and after the conquest.

James A. Michener, *Iberia: Spanish Travels and Reflections*. New York: Random House, 1968. More a charming travelogue than a history, Michener's book reveals the author's gift for explaining the present in terms of the past. Especially interesting is his description of Cortés's homeland.

Eduardo Matos Moctezuma, "The Great Temple," *National Geographic,* vol. 158, no. 6, December 1980. This article describes in detail the building that dominated Tenochtitlán's skyline at the time of the conquest.

August F. Molina Montes, "Tenochtitlán's Glory," *National Geographic,* vol. 158, no. 6, December 1980. Through colorful illustrations, Montes's article explains Aztec building technology.

Henry Bamford Parkes, *A History of Mexico*. Boston: Houghton Mifflin Company, 1960. Parts of Parkes's book describe the friction among the conquistadors and the officials who later came to administer New Spain.

Henry Morton Robinson, *Stout Cortez: A Biography of the Spanish Conquest*. New York: The Century Company, 1931. Written decades before multiculturalism became fashionable, Robinson portrays Cortés as a hero.

Hudson Strode, *Timeless Mexico*. New York: Harcourt, Brace, and Company, 1944. Strode's summary of the Quetzalcoatl myth helps explain why the Aztecs at first viewed the conquistadors as gods.

Gene S. Stuart, *The Mighty Aztecs*. Washington, DC: National Geographic Society, 1981. Filled with colorful illustrations, Stuart's book gives the reader an intriguing look at the greatest American empire before the conquest.

Alpheus Hyatt Verrill, *Great Conquerors of South and Central America*. New York: The New Home Library, 1929. Written when Europeans still saw empire building as a way of civilizing natives, Verrill's book argues that the Spaniards treated their Mexican subjects with astounding compassion and understanding by sixteenth-century standards.

Index

Picture Credits

Cover photo: Stock Montage, Inc.

Archive Photos, 12, 36, 37, 44, 45, 63, 65, 86

Archive Photos/Popperfoto, 29

The Bettmann Archive, 47, 76

Courtesy Department of Library Services, American Museum of Natural History, neg. no. 329239, photo Logan, 60; neg. no. 326597, 69; neg. no. 329240, photo Logan, 81

Giraudon/Art Resource, NY, 88

By permission of the Houghton Library, Harvard University, 31

Laurie Platt Winfrey, Inc., 97

Library of Congress, 13, 41, 95

Mercado/Art Resource, NY, 49, 94

North Wind Picture Archives, 10, 21, 24, 35, 53, 82, 84, 90, 92

Peter Newark's American Pictures, 72

Peter Newark's Western Americana and Historical Pictures, 80

Scala/Art Resource, NY, 25

Sipa Press/Woodfin Camp & Associates, Inc., 17

Stock Montage, Inc., 61, 78

Woodfin Camp & Associates, Inc., 68

About the Author

A native of Elsberry, Missouri, who has taught in public schools for twenty-four years, Stephen R. Lilley holds a master's degree in history. His publishing credits include articles in the *Missouri Historical Review, Missouri Life,* and *Highlights for Children,* and one book, *Hernando Cortes,* published by Lucent Books. He also performs as a traditional jazz musician and has recently released a Dixieland tape, *The Saint Louis Stompers at the Broadway Marina.* Steve and his wife, Becky, have two children, Jacob and Sariya, both of whom are published authors.